Sam Gates is an author, cookery teacher, TV guru and mum. She worked as marketing director of the UK's first food channel before starting her own company, working with clients such as BBC Food, BBC Radio and small food producers. Her first family cookbook, *Food for your Brood*, was published in 2015.

Sam is also a contributor to the *Royal Marsden Cancer Cookbook* and *Liz Earle Wellbeing* magazine, and a regular guest on BBC Radio's *Cook on the Books*. She is a member of the Guild of Food Writers, and runs cooking classes for corporates, schools and charities, teaching toddlers, students, pensioners and the WI how to make sushi.

Sam's second book, *The Tin & Traybake Cookbook* featuring 100 sweet and savoury recipes, was published by Robinson in 2018.

Juggling family, work, life and cooking was the inspiration behind *The Batch Cook Book* and its budget-friendly, low-waste recipes. Sam has been batch cooking since she was a frugal student. Now, as a working mum to a hungry family (and even hungrier rescue dog), it's become a way of life.

Sam – and some of her cooking – can be found on Instagram at @samgatesfood.

Also by Sam Gates

The Tin & Traybake Cookbook

Sam Gates

The Batch Cook Book

WITH PHOTOGRAPHY BY SAM GATES

ROBINSON

ROBINSON

First published in Great Britain in 2020
by Robinson

10 9 8 7 6 5 4 3 2

A CIP catalogue record for this book is available from the British Library.

ISBN 978-1-47214-512-3

Typeset in Alegreya and Alegreya Sans designed by Juan Pablo del Peral

Book designed by Andrew Barron at Thextension

Printed and bound in Great Britain
by Bell & Bain Ltd, Glasgow

Papers used by Robinson are from well-managed forests and other responsible sources.

Robinson
An imprint of
Little, Brown Book Group
Carmelite House
50 Victoria Embankment
London EC4Y 0DZ

An Hachette UK Company
www.hachette.co.uk
www.littlebrown.co.uk

COOK'S NOTES

1 Use salted butter.
2 Use medium-sized eggs, fruit and vegetables unless otherwise specified.
3 Use whole or semi-skimmed milk, but not skimmed.
4 Use fresh herbs unless the recipe calls for dried.
5 Onions and garlic are peeled unless otherwise specified.
6 Wash all vegetables and fruit before use.
7 When cooling rice to store, cool it quickly (within 1 hour), then seal in an airtight container and refrigerate or freeze as soon as possible.

Contents

Acknowledgements

For Mum

Thanks to my lovely, hardworking army of
helpers and recipe testers:

Andrew, Jack, Lulu, Dad, Stefan, Anne, Georgia,
Polly and Daisy, Sally, Annabel, Vicky and Daisy,
Katherine, Carol, Berner, Karen, Katie, John and
Sasha, Natalie, Jess, Emma, Lauren N, Lauren B,
Lucy, Fiona, George, Caroline, Jenny, Mervyn,
Kerry, Izzy.

Huge thanks to my lovely editor Tom Asker,
who believed in this book from the beginning;
the team at Little, Brown: Duncan Proudfoot,
Amanda Keats, Jess Gulliver, Bekki Guyatt and
Abby Marshall; designer Andrew Barron, picture
editor Kasia Fiszer and copyeditor Judy Barratt.

Introduction

Modern batch cooking isn't just about making a vat of bolognese or re-purposing the Christmas turkey. And it's definitely not about complicated shopping lists and strict meal prep calendars that exhaustively dictate when and what you should eat.

Cooking in advance saves time and money as well as helping to reduce waste, and it's more important than ever before. When you need food fast, but the fridge is full of scrag ends and dubious leftovers, your go-to emergency meal might be beans on toast, a packet of fish fingers and frozen peas, or a stash of dried noodles and a bottle of soy sauce. They're all edible and occasionally tasty, but if you're looking for more than just a quick fix for hunger pangs, make-ahead meals are the answer. And there are plenty of other reasons why it's a good idea to make batch cooking and meal prep a regular part of your weekly routine:

Bespoke batches – Batch cooks aren't just for suppers. Batch cook breakfasts if you're not a morning person, stockpile lunches if you're always on the go, or build a helpful cake stash for friends who need tea and sympathy.

Batch basics – Spend a little me-time prepping bases for the freezer. It's quick to transform a classic tomato sauce or a humble white sauce into a delicious meal.

Keep it cosy – Small batches are ideal when you're on your own. Make enough for four and freeze in single portions.

Cook once, eat twice – The batch cook's mantra. Double up your favourite recipe, eat one and freeze the other.

Baby batches – Fill ice-cube trays with simple foods for a ready supply of healthy, tasty food in tiny-tummy-sized portions.

Beautiful batches – Don't be put off by time-consuming, adventurous recipes. Set aside time for a special baking project when you have it, and freeze the results for special occasions.

Cooking for crowds – Want to be in the room where it all happens? Batch cook industrial-sized dishes in advance and you can join the party too.

Batch on track – Need to stay away from certain foods? Stock up on delicious meals that fit the way you want to eat and never feel short-changed by limited offerings.

Above all, planning your meal prep and batch cooks doesn't need to be stressful. Inside this book you'll find more than seventy straight-forward and mouthwatering new recipes that will help you fill your fridge and freezer with delicious meals. All you'll need to do is set aside a little time and enjoy the creative process.

The secret to successful batch cooking is to cook more of what you love when you have the time, so you can eat delicious, fabulous food when you don't!

Money-saving tips – With a little planning, meal prep and batch cooking can make a big difference to your budget.

1   Instead of buying whatever catches your eye on a last-minute supermarket dash, go shopping with recipes in mind and a good idea of the quantities you will need.

2   Buy one-get-one-free offers sound good but if you don't have a plan for those extra ingredients, it can cost you more when they end up in the bin. Include them in batch-cook recipes to ensure nothing is wasted.

3   Seasonal shopping. It doesn't just make environmental sense to buy seasonal produce, it's cheaper too.

4   Buy in bulk. Using the same ingredients in different dishes can make a real difference to your pocket. Tinned foods such as tomatoes, beans and pulses are ideal.

5   Preserve nature's bounty. Forage for wild herbs, hedgerow berries and windfall apples and pears when they are plentiful, and preserve their sweet flavours for leaner days by drying, freezing or stewing.

6   Recycle your leftovers. Use meat and chicken bones, peel and vegetable trimmings to make healthy, preservative-free stocks or turn crusts into breadcrumbs.

7   Store food and ingredients in portion sizes so you can save on waste and defrost only what you need.

The big freeze – The freezer is the batch cook's best friend, a happy place where you can store those home-cooked meals and the single ingredients and bases that kickstart your day-to-day cooking.

Just as it's not worth hoarding clothes, hoping they'll be back on trend one day, it's not worth hanging on to old food either. Start with a ruthless freezer edit, and when the freezer is sparkling clean and ready to fill up, use these helpful tips to keep things running smoothly.

1   Freezers like being full. It makes them run more efficiently, so as soon as it's ready, fill it up!

2   Store liquids, soups, sauces and stews in reusable freezer bags, laid flat and stacked on top of each other. This helps maximise available space, and allows fillings to defrost evenly without getting stuck in those pesky corners.

3   Open freeze meatballs, berries and cookie portions. Lay them flat on a reusable liner on a baking tray and freeze until solid. Then, transfer them to airtight bags or boxes and freeze efficiently.

4   Score traybakes, hash browns and flapjacks into equal slices before freezing. It'll make it easier to remove them from the freezer if you need only a few portions.

5   Label everything! It's tricky to keep track of everything you've cooked, and many frozen foods look alike, so make sure you write names and dates on the packaging before freezing.

6   Freeze in portions. Cut down on waste by dividing your batch cooks into portions for one, two or more so you don't have to defrost more than you need. And if you're cooking for different appetites, add child-sized, adult or extra-hungry labels!

➤➤➤

Batch and prep storage – To help cut down on waste and single-use plastics, try to avoid those traditional food-storage bags that come with little wire ties. From silicone freezer bags, glass boxes and sustainable, compostable packaging to the humble shower cap, you won't have to look too hard to find planet-friendlier alternatives. Here are a few suggestions:

1   Buy self-sealing, good quality bags and re-use them. When they are empty, wash carefully with warm, soapy water and turn inside out to dry.

2   Re-use your other plastic bags and containers. If they don't have air holes, many bread and vegetable bags can be washed and re-used. Every time you do this, it's one less plastic bag in landfill.

3   Invest in reuseable silicone freezer bags, which you can use numerous times before recycling. You can also use them for packed lunches, cupboard storage, and marinating.

4   Use airtight containers, such as Tupperware or Lock & Lock. Buy a stacking set to save on storage space.

5   For large bakes, such as lasagne, line the baking dish with cling film. Place the uncooked bake inside, fold cling film over the top and freeze until just solid. Remove the wrapped bake and slide into a reusable bag for freezing. To cook, remove the cling film and slide it back into the baking dish.

6   Glass Pyrex-style dishes with airtight plastic lids are reusable and excellent for cutting down on washing up! Simply defrost, remove the lid and bake.

7   Silicone muffin moulds create perfect single portions of soups, sauces and sides. Fill the muffin holes and freeze until the contents are solid enough to stack, then tip the portions into bags and boxes.

8   Stock up on extra ice-cube trays and freeze cooking-sized amounts of sauces, wine, gravies and stock.

9   For easy portioning of cakes and bakes, use square and rectangular traybake tins. Score in the tin after baking, then pack and store in layers.

10   Beeswax wraps aren't just reusable, they are compostable too! Use them to wrap sandwiches or to seal dishes for the fridge.

11   Buy a shower cap for the kitchen! Washable plastic shower caps are useful for quick fridge storage. The elastic forms a loose seal around containers, keeping the contents fresh.

Conversion charts

Weight

METRIC	IMPERIAL
25g	1oz
50g	2oz
75g	3oz
100g	4oz
150g	5oz
175g	6oz
200g	7oz
225g	8oz
250g	9oz
300g	10oz
350g	12oz
400g	14oz
450g	1lb

Liquids

METRIC	IMPERIAL	US CUP
5ml	1 tsp	1 tsp
15ml	1 tbsp	1 tbsp
50ml	2fl oz	3 tbsp
60ml	2½fl oz	¼ cup
75ml	3fl oz	⅓ cup
100ml	4fl oz	scant ½ cup
125ml	4½ oz	½ cup
150ml	5fl oz	⅔ cup
200ml	7fl oz	scant 1 cup
250ml	9fl oz	1 cup
300ml	½ pint	1¼ cups
350ml	12fl oz	1⅓ cups
400ml	¾ pint	1¾ cups
500ml	17fl oz	2 cups
600ml	1 pt	2½ cups

Measurements

METRIC	IMPERIAL
5cm	2in
10cm	4in
13cm	5in
15cm	6in
18cm	7in
20cm	8in
25cm	10in
30cm	12in

Oven temperatures

CELSIUS	FAHRENHEIT
110°C	225°F
120°C	250°F
140°C	275°F
150°C	300°F
160°C	325°F
180°C	350°F
190°C	375°F
200°C	400°F
220°C	425°F
230°C	450°F
240°C	475°F

Batch cooking is all about saving time and money as well as reducing waste, and the same applies to prepping your ingredients. Because so many dishes begin with similar foods and flavours, stocking your freezer with a few basics will speed up your meal prep and cooking time even further.

1 | Batch basics

My top batch basics fall into four categories: single ingredients, bases, sauces and flavourbombs. There are plenty of recipes that make use of handy leftovers, such as crusts or the last splash of wine, whilst others are freely foraged or bought and prepared in bulk during seasonal gluts. And as you'll need them often in only small quantities, having a ready-made stash in the freezer is cheaper and more convenient than buying and prepping every time you cook.

We all have our favourite recipes, and no matter how adventurous your cooking, many of those recipes will start with the same combination of ingredients blended into a collection of universal bases and sauces. Then we'll throw in herbs, spices and other flavourings to take them in different directions, perhaps adding oregano to oil, garlic, onions and tomatoes to make a pasta sauce, or cumin and harissa if you're heading towards a vegetable tagine. Because all these dishes start alike, batch cooking a supply of bases for the freezer will save you time when you need to throw a decent meal together fast.

Finally, there are those magical ingredients that you add before serving that really bring a meal to life. It might be a lemon and herb flavourbomb that you stir into a stew at the last minute, a drizzle of red hot chilli oil on a noodle dish, or a knob of fluffy black olive butter run through hot couscous – these late additions are the magic that turns your food from fuel to feast. And you can make them all ahead, which means you can liven up even the most pedestrian food with a cheeky last-minute dose of flavour.

Rather than a lengthy and exhaustive list of shortcuts, this chapter is a shortlist of indispensable batch basics and culinary sparklers that will light up your cooking. Creating them in advance is a brilliant way to get ahead of yourself, so make some space in the freezer, put some awesome music on, pour yourself a drink and get busy. You won't regret it!

Single ingredients

Bread

Don't throw away slightly stale bread or loaf ends. Instead, repurpose them into useful croutons or breadcrumbs. It only takes a minute or two. Croutons add a welcome crunch to soups and salads, and breadcrumbs are ideal for coating fishcakes or patties, adding to meatballs or as a crunchy alternative topping to pastry for your favourite pies.

Croutons

Cut the bread into small cubes. Toss them in a baking tray with a little olive, rapeseed or chilli oil, salt and black pepper and your favourite herbs and spices. Place in the oven at 180°C/160°C fan/Gas mark 4 for 10–12 minutes, turning occasionally until crisp and golden. Allow to cool before storing in freezer bags or airtight boxes. Freeze for up to 2 months.

Breadcrumbs

Tear the bread into large pieces and blitz in a food processor. Tip into freezer bags or airtight boxes. Freeze for up to 2 months.

Wine and gravy ice cubes

A little slurp of wine goes a long way in soups, stews, risottos and gravies. Next time you're lucky enough to have a few inches left in the bottle, pour it into an ice-cube tray and freeze. When the cubes are solid, tip out into freezer bags or airtight boxes, and use as liveners for lacklustre dishes. Do the same with leftover gravies or stocks and add the frozen cubes to sauces and soups.

Herbs

Most fresh herbs grow abundantly in the summer, but die off quickly when autumn appears. Set aside time when your favourite leaves are cheap and plentiful to chop up any excess. Tip into freezer bags or airtight boxes and freeze for up to 3 months. Chives, flat-leaf parsley, coriander, dill and chervil all freeze well.

If you have copious amounts of woody herbs, such as thyme, rosemary or sage, preserve them by hanging them upside down in bunches in a warm place until dry.

Spices

Ready-prepared garlic, ginger and chillies are invaluable when you're short on time, but most jarred versions use taste-altering preservatives. Capture and contain their fabulous flavours more effectively by preparing and freezing the spices yourself.

Using gloves, peel garlic and ginger and finely dice, or chop into large chunks for grating. Deseed and chop fresh chillies. All these spices will keep well in freezer bags or airtight boxes for up to 2 months.

Grated cheese

The ultimate batch basic. Cheese is much cheaper to buy in bulk, so buy the biggest chunks you can afford, grate it yourself and freeze in bags or airtight boxes. You can freeze the cheese in one container, as it's easily portioned into smaller amounts without sticking when you need it. Don't forget to grate and freeze any sad-looking cheeseboard ends, as they'll come in handy too when you need a scattering of cheesy magic.

Fruit

Many fruits keep on giving long after they've lost their looks, especially bananas. You might not want to eat a brown banana, but don't throw them out as they make delicious muffins and cakes. Pop them unpeeled into the freezer, then defrost, peel and use as fresh. Sad apples and pears are useful too. Peel, trim and core, then place in a saucepan with a little water and cook until they form a rough mush. Blitz for a few seconds in a food processor if you want a smoother purée. Freeze for up to 3 months.

No one likes a soggy berry, and I find that if we don't eat them immediately, they tend to end up with a one-way ticket to the bin. But catch them in time and they're perfect for crumbles, smoothies and cakes. Place excess or unwanted berries in a single layer on a baking tray and open freeze for 1–2 hours, or until they are hard enough to be stored in a freezer bag or box without squashing each other. Freeze for up to 3 months.

Bases

Most stew, curry, soup and casserole recipes begin with heating oil or butter and gently frying a few chopped onions with whichever herbs and spices that particular cuisine uses for its distinctive flavours. Chopping these ingredients is usually the only fiddly part of the recipe, and once that's done, you'll just need to add vegetables, meat, fish or grains and liquids to create the final dish.

You can freeze all the bases below. When you want to cook, defrost your chosen base over a gentle heat and you're away. Each recipe makes enough to fill a standard ice-cube tray or several small airtight containers. All the bases in this section can be frozen in a standard ice-cube tray or small, airtight containers. When you're ready to cook, defrost your chosen base over a gentle heat and add your favourite ingredients, or use it to make one of the simple recipes below.

Thai base

6 tbsp groundnut or vegetable oil,
    plus extra for covering
large bunch of coriander, stalks and
    leaves chopped
4 garlic cloves, crushed
2 shallots, chopped
3 tbsp grated fresh ginger
2 red chillies, deseeded and chopped
2 lemongrass stalks, trimmed and very
    finely chopped

6 kaffir lime leaves, stems removed and
    very finely chopped
finely grated zest and juice of 1 lime
1 tbsp fish sauce

Place all the ingredients into a mini food processor and blitz to a smooth paste. Spoon the paste into the ice-cube tray to just below the top of each hollow. Drizzle a thin layer of oil over the top of each one. Place the tray on to a small baking tray and place in the freezer. Freeze for 1–2 hours until the cubes are firm enough to hold their shape, before storing in freezer bags or airtight boxes. Here's a recipe suggestion that serves 3–4 people:

Simple Thai curry

Warm 1 tablespoon of vegetable oil in a wok or deep frying pan and add 2 defrosted cubes of Thai base. Fry quickly for 2–3 minutes until the paste is cooked, then add 400ml coconut milk and 400ml chicken or vegetable stock. Simmer until piping hot and add 600g bite-sized pieces of chicken, seafood or vegetables. Continue simmering until cooked through. Add soy sauce to taste and scatter with coriander leaves before serving.

Garlic and herb base

8 tbsp olive oil, plus extra for covering
stalks from a large bunch of basil, finely chopped
2 onions, finely chopped
4 garlic cloves, crushed
1 tsp dried oregano
salt and black pepper to season

Place all the ingredients except the seasoning into a frying pan and gently sauté for 6–8 minutes until soft. Season generously with salt and pepper. Spoon the paste into the ice-cube tray to just below the top of each hollow. Drizzle a thin layer of oil over the top of each one. Place the tray on to a small baking tray and place in the freezer. Freeze for 1–2 hours until the cubes are firm enough to hold their shape, before storing in freezer bags or airtight boxes. Here's a recipe idea for your garlic and herb base that serves 4:

Tomato and basil pasta sauce

Place 1 tablespoon of olive oil and 2 defrosted cubes of garlic-and-herb base into a heavy-bottomed saucepan. Cook for 3 minutes until hot, then add 2 tins of chopped tomatoes and 1 tablespoon of tomato purée. Bring to a gentle simmer and cook for 20 minutes. Add a little water if the mixture is too thick. Just before serving, taste and season with salt and pepper. Stir in 2 handfuls of basil leaves, torn into small pieces. Toss through hot pasta and scatter with Parmesan cheese.

Winter soup base

4 tbsp olive oil, plus extra for covering
40g butter
3 small onions, finely chopped
3 carrots, finely chopped
4 leeks, quartered lengthways and finely chopped
4 celery sticks, finely diced
large bunch of flat-leaf parsley, stalks and leaves finely chopped
1 tbsp thyme leaves
salt and black pepper to season

Place all the ingredients except the seasoning into a frying pan and gently sauté until soft. Season generously with salt and pepper, and cool. Divide the base between 4 small airtight boxes, and cover each with a thin layer of oil. Seal and freeze for up to 2 months. Here's a recipe idea for your winter soup base that serves 4:

Curried root vegetable soup

Add 1 portion of defrosted soup base to a heavy-bottomed saucepan and heat through. Add half a teaspoon of curry powder and stir for 2 minutes. Pour in 750ml chicken or vegetable stock and bring to the boil. Add 500g peeled, roughly chopped parsnips and cook for 15–20 minutes until soft. Blitz until smooth and season to taste with salt and pepper.

Wild mushroom base

If you're lucky enough to find more edible wild mushrooms than you can eat, this is a wonderful way to preserve them. It does seem like a lot of butter, and a long cooking time, but undercooked mushrooms are horrid, so it's worth giving them all the time they need.

120g butter
4 shallots, finely chopped
4 garlic cloves, crushed
bunch of flat-leaf parsley, stalks and leaves
    chopped separately
1kg wild or cultivated mushrooms, thinly sliced
1 tsp Maldon salt, plus extra to season
black pepper to season

Melt the butter in a large, deep frying pan and gently fry the shallots, garlic and parsley stalks for 6–8 minutes until soft. Add the mushrooms and the salt and cook gently for 20 minutes until the mushrooms are slightly golden and any liquid is completely reduced. Stir in the parsley leaves, season to taste with salt and pepper and allow to cool. Divide the base between 4 small airtight boxes, and cover each with a thin layer of oil. Seal and freeze for up to 2 months. Here's a recipe idea for your wild mushroom base that serves 2:

Wild mushroom pasta

Defrost 1 portion of wild mushroom base. Gently warm it through in a frying pan. Add 4 tablespoons of double cream and heat through. Add more salt and pepper if needed and toss through hot pasta. Drizzle with olive or truffle oil before serving.

Sauces

These are my top three sauces. They are all big-hearted multi-taskers, which you can use to form the base of myriad dishes. Make a big vat of each for the freezer, and you'll never be far from a gorgeous meal.

Rich tomato sauce

This sauce is a luxurious blank canvas. Just add your favourite herbs and spices to take it in whichever culinary direction you like, whether it's oregano and bay for a mild pasta sauce, or cumin and fresh chillies for North African stew. And for the days when you're too tired to even think about cooking, just ladle some straight into a mug, scatter grated cheese over the top and sip it greedily, whilst wrapped in a blanket on the sofa. Feeds 8 as a pasta sauce, easily halved or doubled.

5 tbsp olive oil
2 red onions, finely diced
3 large garlic cloves, crushed
1 carrot, peeled and finely diced
2 celery sticks, finely diced
4 x 400g tins of chopped tomatoes
1 tbsp tomato purée
1 tsp caster sugar
salt and black pepper to season

Gently heat the oil in a saucepan and sauté the onions, garlic, carrot and celery for 10–12 minutes until softened. Stir in the tomatoes, purée and sugar and season generously with salt and pepper. Bring to the boil and turn down to a gentle simmer. Partially cover and cook, stirring regularly, for 30 minutes, until the sauce is rich and thick. Taste and add more seasoning if needed. Allow to cool completely before storing in the fridge for up to three days or in the freezer for up to 2 months.

Chilli sauce

A punchy, lighter version of a popular high-street chilli sauce. Add to stir-fried meat, fish and veggies or mix with rice or noodles. It's also a great dipping sauce. Makes enough stir-fry sauce for 8.

2 tsp vegetable oil
4 lemongrass stalks, trimmed and very finely chopped
2 large thumb-sized pieces of fresh ginger, peeled and finely chopped
2 large red chillies, trimmed and finely chopped
1 large red onion, finely chopped
1 carrot, peeled and very finely chopped
4 garlic cloves, crushed
1 tsp salt
2 tbsp light soy sauce
2 red peppers, fresh or drained from a jar, trimmed, deseeded and finely chopped
1 tsp rice vinegar
1 tsp fish sauce
2 tbsp tomato purée

Heat the oil in a saucepan and add the lemongrass, ginger, chillies, onion, carrot, garlic, salt and soy sauce. Fry gently for 10 minutes until the onion is soft, but not browned. Add the peppers and continue cooking for another 10 minutes. Remove from the heat and stir in the vinegar, fish sauce, tomato purée and 600ml of water. Bring to the boil, then turn down the heat and simmer gently for another 10 minutes. Liquidise until smooth. Allow to cool completely before freezing for up to 2 months. Defrost completely before using.

White sauce

Use this simple white sauce as a base for pour-over and cook-in sauces. Make a batch and freeze it in portions, then defrost it as needed, before reheating gently and adding your favourite cheeses, herbs, mustards or spices. Makes 1 litre of sauce and is easily doubled for bigger batches.

80g butter
80g plain flour
1 litre milk
salt and black pepper to season

Melt the butter with the flour, stirring until the mixture forms a tan-coloured paste. Add the milk a little at a time, whisking continuously. Bring gently to the boil, stirring until the sauce has thickened. Season with salt and pepper to taste. Cover with a lid and allow to cool completely before freezing for up to 2 months.

Flavourbombs

These unassuming extras are simple to throw together, but their sneaky, power-packed flavours will take your food to a whole new level of deliciousness.

Garlic, lemon and herb

This is a fabulously effective chef's trick for livening dishes. Make the flavourbomb and stir it through stews and casseroles just before serving. The lemon and herbs sharpen and intensify flavours without dominating. This recipe makes one flavourbomb but you can multiply and freeze it in ice-cube trays with a layer of olive oil drizzled over the top.

finely grated zest of 1 lemon
1 garlic clove, finely chopped
handful of finely chopped flat-leaf parsley leaves
1 tsp finely chopped rosemary leaves
2 tsp olive oil, plus extra for drizzling
salt and black pepper to season

Mix the lemon zest, garlic, parsley, rosemary and olive oil together in a small bowl. Season with salt and pepper and mix well.

Green pepper and caraway

I originally made this to use up a green-chilli surfeit, but now make it all the time. Use as a side, sauce or salsa, or tossed through grains, beans, lentils or couscous. Cover with a thin drizzle of oil to freeze. Makes enough to fill a standard ice-cube tray.

2 tsp black peppercorns
2 tsp coriander seeds
2 tsp caraway seeds
1 tsp cumin seeds
seeds from 6 cardamom pods
5 green chillies, trimmed, deseeded and
    roughly chopped
1 green pepper, deseeded and diced
1 large bunch of flat-leaf parsley, leaves picked
1 large bunch of coriander, leaves picked
3 garlic cloves, roughly chopped
½ tsp salt
6 tbsp olive oil, plus extra for drizzling
2 tbsp lemon juice

Dry roast the peppercorns, coriander, caraway, cumin and cardamom seeds lightly in a small frying pan on a medium heat for 2 minutes. Finely crush or grind the roasted spices in a pestle and mortar or spice grinder.

Place the spices into a small food processor with the remaining ingredients and blitz for a couple of seconds until you have a rough paste.

Wild garlic oil

Wild garlic is virtually impossible to find out
of season, which makes it even more special.
Extend its life span with these frozen cubes, and
use them in place of straight olive oil as a base
for soups, stews and sauces.

300ml olive oil, plus extra for covering
50g young wild garlic leaves, finely chopped
salt and black pepper to season

Mix the olive oil and chopped wild garlic and
season well. Pour into ice-cube trays, cover with
a thin layer of oil and freeze. To use, tip into a
saucepan and warm gently.

Red hot chilli oil

Chilli oil brings heat and colour to many recipes,
especially when drizzled over just before serving.
Making your own is quick and easy, and it will
keep for up to 1 month in a cool, dark place.
You will need a sterilised 500ml bottle.

460ml olive oil
4 dried red chillies
3 tbsp red chilli flakes

Heat the oil in a small saucepan on a medium heat
until hot but not boiling or smoking. Add the
whole chillies and the chilli flakes and warm for
4 minutes. Allow to cool, pour into the sterilised
bottle and leave to infuse for 12–24 hours. Strain
the oil and return to the bottle, adding the whole
chillies for decoration if desired.

Whipped butters

Whipping butter takes it to a new and infinitely
fluffier dimension, and it's divine on hot toast,
melted on fish, meat or vegetables, or tossed
through a bowl of pasta. Experiment with
different flavours by adding your favourite
ingredients, herbs, spices and seasoning, or
try out the recipes that follow.

Garlic and herb butter

100g butter, softened
2 garlic cloves, crushed
2 tbsp chopped flat-leaf parsley
salt and black pepper to season

Black olive and thyme

100g butter, softened
8 pitted black olives, finely chopped
1 garlic clove, crushed
salt and black pepper to season

Horseradish and dill

100g butter, softened
20g dill, finely chopped
1 tbsp creamed horseradish
salt and black pepper to season

Coriander and lime

100g butter, softened
20g coriander, finely chopped
finely grated zest of 1 lime
salt and black pepper to season

Blue cheese and chive

100g butter, softened
20g chives, finely chopped
30g soft blue cheese
salt and black pepper to season

Sun-dried tomato and thyme

100g butter, softened
8 sun-dried tomatoes, finely chopped
¼ tsp finely chopped thyme leaves
salt and black pepper to season

Place the ingredients into a bowl or stand mixer
and whisk until the butter becomes pale and
fluffy. Season with salt and pepper to taste.
Keep in the fridge for 3 days or freeze in airtight
containers.

For most of us, breakfast is either the most hurried meal of the day, or the one we're most likely to skip. Give these batch-cooked breakfasts a try and you'll soon fall in love with longer lie-ins, calmer mornings and energy that will last you until lunchtime.

2 | Breakfasts — the best batch of the day

BREAKFAST
BEAN BURRITOS

BREAKFAST

Perfect households, which run smoothly on well-organised, super-efficient morning schedules, do exist somewhere, I'm sure. In these happy homes, the breakfast table will have been laid the night before, school and work bags sorted and pre-packed, tidy and nutritionally balanced lunches wait obediently in the fridge and there is a wonderful sense of calm and well-being that permeates the house and sets everyone up beautifully for the day ahead.

But for most busy families, morning reality is usually noisier, messier and a lot more chaotic. Our house was a perfect example. Each day the walls resonated with the sounds of reluctant sleepers being turfed out of bed, clomping up and down stairs, bags flying, people scrambling to find lost clothing, panic packing and repeated attempts to leave the building. Managing to get a little cereal into reluctant kids before leaving with a half-eaten piece of toast in one hand and everything else in the other was considered a big success. We were happy, but without a proper breakfast, starting every day in a hungry, frantic rush was exhausting.

Discovering breakfast batches was a revelation, especially as it's possible to make so many great breakfast recipes in advance. As we began experimenting with new dishes, these make-ahead meals became our family's ticket to a better-fed, gentler and all-round less stressful start to the day.

In this chapter you'll find recipes for twelve beautiful breakfasts to make in advance, from crunchy homemade granola and classic muffins that resourcefully use up past-their-best freezer bananas, to spicy shakshuka portions and oven-ready bean burritos to warm up while you get your act together. And if you love your lie-ins, but have a celebratory morning coming up that demands something special, why not treat yourself to a relaxing baking session and make a majestic breakfast couronne for the freezer?

Breakfast may be the most important meal of the day but it's more likely to be the time of day when we have no time at all. Cooking ahead can help, so get your batch on and set yourself up for a stress-free start to the day!

The best batch breakfasts

Cranberry, pistachio and marzipan swirly buns

Spiced orange, sour cherry and pecan couronne

Frozen banana and walnut muffins

Salted honey flapjacks with almonds and figs

Apple and cinnamon toaster waffles

DIY honey-roasted granola

Smoky bean breakfast burritos

Big batch spinach and potato hash browns

Chorizo, chilli and squash quesadillas

Seeded buttermilk no-knead loaf with whipped Marmite butter

Cheese, chive and ham hock scones

Perfectly portioned shakshuka

Cranberry, pistachio and marzipan swirly buns

Bake these ridiculously luxurious buns when you really want to spoil yourself or someone very special. They are made with a soft and pillowy enriched dough, filled with marzipan and cranberries, and perfumed with orange. It's a good way to use up any leftover Christmas marzipan or dried fruit and your kitchen will smell heavenly!

MAKES 16

FOR THE DOUGH
14g easy dried yeast
300ml lukewarm milk
80g caster sugar
500g strong white bread flour, plus extra
    for dusting
big pinch of salt
100g butter, melted
1 egg, beaten

FOR THE FILLING AND GLAZE
100g caster sugar
100g butter, softened
100g dried cranberries, chopped
40g pistachios, chopped
200g marzipan, finely diced
finely grated zest of 1 orange
1 egg, beaten

1 Mix the yeast with the warm milk and 1 teaspoon of the sugar, then cover and leave for 15 minutes until frothy.

2 Tip the remaining sugar into a large mixing bowl with the flour and salt. Pour in the melted butter, beaten egg and the frothy, milky yeast and mix well. Knead the dough until it becomes smooth and less sticky, then cover and leave to rise for 30 minutes somewhere warm.

3 While it's rising, make the filling. Set aside 3 tablespoons of sugar for the glaze, then tip the rest into a small bowl and add the softened butter. Beat together, then stir in the chopped cranberries until you have a paste.

4 When the dough has risen, tip it on to a floured work surface and knead it lightly. Transfer to a large piece of greaseproof paper and roll it out into a large rectangle about 40cm x 30cm.

5 Set aside a tablespoon of chopped pistachios for serving. Spread the paste over the dough and scatter with the remaining pistachios and the marzipan. Sprinkle the orange zest evenly over the top.

6 Lift the longest side of the dough and roll it into a large log shape with the filling swirled inside. Carefully cut it into 16 even slices without squashing the log. Place the slices on 2 baking trays lined with greaseproof paper or reusable liners. Cover and leave to rise somewhere warm for another 30 minutes.

7 Preheat the oven to 190°C/170°C fan/ Gas mark 5.

8 Brush the buns with beaten egg and bake for 20–22 minutes, until they are beautifully golden on top. In the last few minutes of baking, heat the reserved 3 tablespoons of sugar with 2 tablespoons of water until it boils, then remove from the heat. Remove the buns from the oven and paint with the sugar glaze. Sprinkle with the reserved pistachios, to serve.

TO FREEZE
Cool the buns completely and wrap them in greaseproof paper or cling film. Freeze for up to 3 months. To reheat, defrost completely, remove the wrapping and reheat in the microwave for a few seconds.

Spiced orange, sour cherry and pecan couronne

Make-ahead recipes are a lifesaver when it comes to preparing food in advance of busy days, but they're also a great way to make sure you have a showstopper up your sleeve for significant events. This majestic fruit couronne freezes well and is brilliant for birthdays or important mornings when the occasion calls for something special. The recipe is made in stages, so it's ideal for a weekend baking project.

FEEDS 6—8

FOR THE DOUGH

250g strong white bread flour, plus extra
    for mixing
7g easy dried yeast
2 tbsp dark brown soft sugar
½ tsp mixed spice
finely grated zest and juice of 2 oranges
50g butter, softened
1 egg, beaten
80ml lukewarm milk

FOR THE FILLING AND GLAZE

60g dried sour cherries, halved
70g sultanas
80g butter
60g dark brown soft sugar
30g plain flour
50g pecan nuts, chopped
2 tbsp caster sugar

1 Mix the flour, yeast, sugar, mixed spice and orange zest (saving the juice) together in a large bowl. Rub in the butter until the mixture looks like fine breadcrumbs, then add the beaten egg and milk. Using a flat-bladed knife, stir until everything starts to come together.

2 Flour your hands and worktop, and tip out the dough. Knead, using a little more flour if needed, until the dough feels smooth and flexible. Place it back in the bowl, cover with greased cling film or a greased, tight-fitting lid and leave to rise somewhere warm for 1–2 hours until doubled in size.

3 While it's rising, make the filling. Place the cherries, sultanas and reserved orange juice (from the dough recipe) into a small saucepan. Bring to the boil, remove from the heat and leave to cool for 1 hour. Strain and reserve the liquid for glazing the couronne.

4 Beat the butter and sugar together until fluffy. Mix in the flour and the drained fruit. Set aside 1 tablespoon of chopped pecan nuts and stir the rest into the mixture.

5 When the dough is ready, place a sheet of greaseproof paper approximately 70cm long on a work surface. Place the dough on top and roll it out into a 30cm x 20cm rectangle. Spread the filling evenly over the dough.

➤➤➤

6 Carefully lift up the longest side of the paper and start rolling the dough into a long cylinder, as if you were making a Swiss roll, tucking in any errant fruits as you roll. With floured hands, rock and roll it gently backwards and forwards, without squashing the cylinder, until it is 55–60cm long.

7 Cut the cylinder in half lengthways, and let each side fall flat, so that the cut sides are exposed. Starting at one end, place one cut side over the other, then repeat until the two pieces are twisted together into a two-strand plait. Bring the ends around to meet each other, and press them together to make a 'crown'. Gently push in any dried fruit sticking out of the flour, so that it doesn't burn while baking. Lift the paper and crown on to a large baking tray, cover with greased cling film and leave to prove for 1 hour somewhere warm.

8 Preheat the oven to 170°C/150°C fan/Gas mark 3. Remove the cling film and bake the couronne for 20 minutes, then turn up the heat to 180°C/160°C fan/Gas mark 4 and cover the couronne loosely with foil. Bake for another 15 minutes until well risen and golden. Remove from the oven and set aside.

9 Quickly heat the strained dried fruit liquid with the caster sugar in a small pan until it boils and thickens into a syrup. Remove from the heat and brush the syrup over the couronne. It will dry quickly into a shiny glaze. Scatter with the remaining chopped pecan nuts and serve immediately.

TO FREEZE

Cool completely, wrap in foil and freeze for up to 3 months. To serve, preheat the oven to 170°C/150°C fan/Gas mark 3. Loosen the foil slightly and place the couronne on a baking tray. Heat for 15–20 minutes until warmed through.

Frozen banana and walnut muffins

Banana muffins are a much-loved breakfast treat and this nutty, spicy version is delicious and quick to knock together. Frozen bananas are brilliant for baking and they defrost quickly, so whenever you find yourself with dodgy-looking bananas, pop them in the freezer. This recipe also works just as well with fresh bananas. Best of all, you can freeze any uneaten muffins for those moments when only a muffin will do.

MAKES 12

260g plain flour
1 tsp bicarbonate of soda
1 tsp baking powder
¼ tsp salt
½ tsp ground cinnamon
3 large ripe or defrosted bananas, mashed
120g light brown soft sugar
2 eggs, beaten
5 tbsp milk
90ml sunflower oil
½ tsp vanilla essence
50g walnuts, chopped, plus extra to decorate

1   Preheat the oven to 190°C/170°C fan/Gas mark 5 and place 12 muffin cases into a 12-hole muffin tin.

2   Mix the flour, bicarbonate of soda, baking powder, salt and cinnamon in a large mixing bowl.

3   In another bowl, mix the mashed bananas, sugar, eggs, milk, oil and vanilla essence.

4   Pour the banana mixture into the dry ingredients and mix briefly until you can't see any streaks of flour but the mixture is still lumpy. Fold through the chopped walnuts.

5   Pour the batter equally into the muffin cases and sprinkle over the extra chopped walnuts. Bake for 20–25 minutes until the tops spring back up when lightly pressed.

TO FREEZE
Cool completely, seal in an airtight box or bag and freeze for up to 3 months. Defrost and reheat for 10–20 seconds in the microwave until warm through. To reheat from frozen, loosely wrap in foil and place in a preheated oven at 150°C/110°C fan/Gas mark 2 for 10–12 minutes until piping hot.

Salted honey flapjacks with almonds and figs

Salt and honey work beautifully together in these super-sweet crunchy bars. They are ideal for a grab-and-go breakfast when there is a seriously busy morning ahead or you just know you're going to need a naughty mid-morning treat. If you have a glut of ripe figs, make a big batch for the freezer and you can enjoy their glorious sun-kissed flavour long after summer is over.

MAKES 20–25

250g fresh figs
200g light brown soft sugar
finely grated zest and juice of 1 lemon
200g butter
200g runny honey
1 tsp Maldon salt, crumbled
2 tbsp finely grated fresh ginger
450g porridge oats (not jumbo oats)
80g flaked almonds

1   Preheat the oven to 180°C/160°C fan/ Gas mark 4 and grease and line a 35cm x 25cm traybake tin with greaseproof paper or a reusable liner.

2   Set aside 3 figs (approximately 100g) to decorate the top of the flapjacks. Roughly chop the remaining figs and place them in a bowl with 50g of the sugar and all the lemon zest and juice.

3   Place the remaining sugar in a large saucepan with the butter, honey, salt and ginger, and warm gently until the sugar has completely dissolved.

4   Remove from the heat and stir in the oats, almonds and chopped figs, including any juices. Pour the mixture into the prepared baking tin and smooth flat.

5   Slice the remaining whole figs horizontally into thin slices and lay the slices on top of the flapjack mixture. Bake for 40–45 minutes, until the flapjack starts to turn a dark golden brown around the edges of the tin.

6   Remove from the oven, and cool for 15 minutes before turning out and cutting into generous slices.

TO FREEZE
Cool completely, wrap the flapjacks between sheets of greaseproof paper and seal in freezer bags or airtight containers for up to 1 month.

Apple and cinnamon toaster waffles

Waffles are always delicious at fairs and festivals, especially when they're served up with a wiggly squeeze of cream and caramel sauce. But with well-priced waffle irons readily available, they are just as easy to make at home. Just remember that, as with pancakes, the first couple of waffles won't be the best, so consider them to be the cook's treat and move on swiftly. This is a simple batter recipe in which the apple and cinnamon flavours are beautifully balanced. For breakfast, they are perfect just as they are, but you can also add ice cream and yummy sweet things to turn them into quick puddings

MAKES 8–10

150g butter
3 eggs, separated
120g caster sugar, plus extra for serving
300g plain flour
1½ tsp baking powder
2 tsp ground cinnamon
300ml milk
½ tsp vanilla essence
2 eating apples, peeled, cored and grated
sunflower oil, for greasing

1   Using a hand mixer, beat the butter until light and fluffy, then add the egg yolks and sugar alternately in batches, mixing well between each addition until the mixture is completely combined.

2   Mix together the flour, baking powder and cinnamon in a small bowl, then gradually add the dry mixture to the butter and sugar mixture, stirring between each addition.

3   Mix the milk and vanilla essence in a jug and slowly beat it into the batter. Stir through the grated apples.

4   In a separate bowl, beat the egg whites until they form stiff peaks, then gently fold them into the batter, trying to keep as much volume as possible. Place in the fridge until ready to cook.

5   Waffle iron instructions may vary according to manufacturer and size, so the following is a general cooking guide only.

6   Grease the plates of your waffle iron with a light coating of oil. Heat the waffle iron and add the manufacturer's suggested quantity of batter to the centre of the lower waffle plate. Lower the upper plate and cook the waffle until it reaches the desired colour.

7   When the waffle is ready, dust with a little more caster sugar and serve hot. Repeat with the remaining mixture, turning off the iron to brush with more oil if needed.

TO FREEZE
Cool completely and do not dust with sugar. Stack the waffles between layers of greaseproof paper. Seal in a bag or airtight box and freeze for up to 1 month. Reheat briefly in a toaster and dust with sugar before serving if desired.

DIY honey-roasted granola

The best thing about homemade granola is that you can adjust the ingredients to your taste. Hate raisins? Leave them out! Love almonds? Add more! This recipe has plenty of both, but it's very forgiving, so feel free to substitute your favourite alternatives. Just do try to include cranberries or dried sour cherries as they bring welcome colour to the granola as well as a delicious tart sweetness. This is a big, brassy batch recipe, which makes around 1.3kg of crunchy golden granola. You can halve the ingredients if you prefer to make less, just keep a close eye on the oven, as it will need less cooking time.

500g jumbo oats
250g mixed nuts (walnuts, hazelnuts
    and almonds), chopped
140g mixed seeds
60g coconut oil
180g runny honey
2 tsp Maldon salt
½ tsp ground cinnamon
70g raisins or sultanas
50g dried apricots, chopped
50g cranberries

1   Preheat the oven to 150°C/130°C fan/Gas mark 2 and line a large baking tray with greaseproof paper.

2   Mix the oats, nuts and mixed seeds together in a large mixing bowl.

3   In a small pan, heat the coconut oil, honey, salt and cinnamon, and stir until it's completely combined. Allow to cool for a few minutes, then pour the mixture over the oats and nuts. Mix thoroughly, and then tip out on to the lined baking tray. Use a spatula to smooth it down roughly.

4   Bake for 35–45 minutes, turning over every 10–15 minutes so that it is evenly baked.

5   Remove from the oven, stir well and mix in the dried fruit. Allow to cool completely before storing in airtight containers for up to 2 months.

Smoky bean breakfast burritos

Oh so much better than beans on toast! These thick breakfast burritos are packed with smoky-sweet fiery flavours and oozy cheese. Perhaps they're a little generous for a simple weekday breakfast, but they're definitely the answer when you're after serious fuel to fortify you for a big day, or need to rectify the after-effects of a big night out. Swap the cheddar for vegan cheese if you don't do dairy.

MAKES 8

2 tbsp olive oil, plus extra for brushing
2 onions, finely chopped
1 celery stick, finely chopped
1 large carrot, peeled and coarsely grated
1 red chilli, deseeded and finely chopped
1 green pepper, deseeded and diced
1 yellow pepper, deseeded and diced
½ tsp ground cumin
1 tsp smoked paprika
3 tbsp tomato purée
1 tsp granulated sugar
1 x 400g tin of chopped tomatoes
2 x 400g tins of mixed beans, drained
8 large flour tortillas
4 handfuls of baby spinach
200g mature cheddar, grated
salt and black pepper to season

1 Heat the oil in a large, heavy-based saucepan and gently cook the onions, celery, carrot and chilli for 10–12 minutes until softened.

2 Add the peppers, cumin and smoked paprika and cook for 4 minutes. Season well and stir in the tomato purée and sugar. Pour in the tinned tomatoes, drained beans and half a tin of water.

3 Bring to the boil, then stir and reduce the heat to a gentle simmer. Cook for 20–30 minutes until thick, rich and syrupy. Turn off the heat and roughly mash the beans so the mixture holds together. If it is still watery, cook for a little longer. Season to taste and allow to cool before making the burritos.

4 Lay out a large tortilla and place a layer of baby spinach on the half closest to you. Spoon an eighth of the bean mixture in a rectangle in the centre and cover with an eighth of the grated cheddar.

5 Fold in the sides of the tortilla and hold them in as you start rolling from the side closest to you. Finish with the seam side downwards, and repeat with the rest of the tortillas. Brush with a little oil on both sides.

6 Heat a little oil in a frying pan and fry each burrito on each side for 4–5 minutes until lightly golden.

TO FREEZE
Allow to cool and wrap tightly in foil. Freeze in an airtight container or bag for up to 1 month.

TO REHEAT
Defrost without unwrapping and place on a baking tray in a preheated oven at 180°C/160°C fan/Gas mark 4 for 20 minutes until piping hot. Alternatively, you can cook the burritos from frozen at the same temperature for 35–40 minutes.

Big batch spinach and potato hash browns

Hash browns are a gorgeously golden alternative to toast as a sturdy base for poached or fried eggs as well as bacon, tomatoes and other traditional breakfast staples. This gluten-free recipe makes a large batch, which will be useful as they disappear very fast! It's a good recipe to make in advance, because you can cook the hash browns straight from the freezer. If you prefer, you can make them with oil instead of butter.

MAKES 16

1kg unpeeled potatoes
1 large Spanish onion, finely sliced
40g butter
¼ tsp paprika
100g spinach, roughly chopped
salt and black pepper to season
vegetable oil for frying, to serve

1 Line a roasting or traybake tin measuring approximately 23cm x 30cm with greaseproof paper or a reusable liner.

2 Place the unpeeled potatoes in a large saucepan of cold water (cutting any very large potatoes in half) and bring to the boil. Boil for 10 minutes, then drain and leave to cool.

3 Meanwhile, fry the onion slowly in a frying pan with the butter, paprika and a large pinch of salt for 10–15 minutes until soft but not brown. Stir through the chopped spinach until it wilts, then tip the mixture into a large mixing bowl.

4 When the potatoes are cool, grate them into the mixing bowl. The skins will slide off – you can discard them. Season very generously with salt and pepper, mix well, then tip the mixture into the lined tin and smooth evenly.

5 Score the mixture into 16 pieces. (See freezer notes now if you intend to freeze.)

6 To cook, heat a tablespoon of oil in a non-stick frying pan until hot. Place 4 hash browns in the pan at a time and cook on a medium heat for 5–7 minutes each side, moving them around as little as possible until they are crispy and piping hot.

TO FREEZE
Place the scored hash browns, uncovered, in the freezer, for 40–50 minutes until solid. Remove the tray from the freezer and place the hash browns in layers of foil or greaseproof paper. Place in an airtight box or bag and freeze for up to 2 months.

TO COOK
Heat 1 tablespoon of oil in a non-stick frying pan until hot. Place 4 defrosted hash browns in the pan and cook on a medium heat for 5–7 minutes each side, moving as little as possible until crispy and piping hot. If cooking from frozen, they will need 10–12 minutes on each side.

Chorizo, chilli and squash quesadillas

Fiery quesadillas are a great breakfast option when you need to blast away the cobwebs. The filling is a nice balance of sweet, caramelised squash, fiery chorizo and cool mint. If you like your flavours extra hot, choose a very spicy chorizo. This filling is great with traditional white-flour tortillas, or brightly multi-coloured spinach or beetroot wraps. The filling will keep for 2 days in the fridge.

FEEDS 4

750g butternut squash, peeled, deseeded and
    chopped into 1cm chunks
2 tbsp olive oil, plus extra for frying
1 red chilli, deseeded and finely chopped
100g baby spinach
100g chorizo, quartered lengthways and
    chopped into small pieces
8 tortilla wraps
120g mozzarella or cheddar, grated
2 tbsp chopped fresh mint leaves
salt and black pepper to season

1 Preheat the oven to 180°C/160°C fan/
Gas mark 4.

2 Place the butternut chunks in a baking tin and mix with the oil and chopped chilli. Season well and roast, stirring occasionally, for 40 minutes, until it starts to brown around the edges.

3 Remove from the oven and tip into a bowl with any oil from the tin. Roughly crush the squash and toss with the baby spinach leaves straight away so they wilt in the heat. Set aside.

4 Fry the chorizo in a small frying pan, and when it's nicely crispy, tip into the squash and spinach mixture.

5 Warm 1 tablespoon of olive oil in a large frying pan over a medium heat. Place a tortilla flat in the frying pan, spoon in a quarter of the squash mixture and spread it evenly over the tortilla. Sprinkle over a quarter of the cheese.

6 Place another tortilla over the top, and press down gently. Cook for 3–4 minutes until warmed through and the cheese has melted. Use a spatula to gently peek under the edges to check it is not burning.

7 When the base is nicely golden, carefully turn the quesadilla over and cook the other side. Remove from the pan and keep warm. Repeat the process with the remaining quesadillas. To serve, sprinkle with fresh mint and cut into triangles with a pizza cutter.

MAKE AHEAD
Make the squash filling up to 2 days in advance, cool completely and store in the fridge until required.

Seeded buttermilk no-knead loaf with whipped Marmite butter

The idea of a beautiful loaf made without kneading sounds unlikely, but this seeded buttermilk bread asks nothing more of the cook than to be mixed and baked. It has a gentle, slightly cake-like texture and tastes amazing warm from the oven or lightly toasted. If you're a Marmite lover, whip up some of this butter too, and you'll be lucky if the loaf lasts a morning.

1 tbsp runny honey
284ml buttermilk
1 egg, beaten
3 tbsp sunflower oil
1½ tsp baking powder
½ tsp bicarbonate of soda
1 tsp salt
330g plain flour
4 tbsp mixed seeds, plus extra
    for sprinkling

FOR THE WHIPPED MARMITE BUTTER
100g butter, softened
1½ tbsp Marmite

1 Preheat the oven to 180°C/160°C fan/Gas mark 4 and line a large loaf tin with greaseproof paper or a reusable liner.

2 Make the loaf. Place the honey, buttermilk, beaten egg and oil in a large bowl and mix. Stir the baking powder, bicarbonate of soda, salt, flour and seeds together in another bowl, and then tip them into the buttermilk mixture. Stir until just combined and you can't see any flour streaks.

3 Pour into the lined loaf tin and sprinkle with a few extra seeds. Bake for 40–45 minutes until a skewer inserted into the centre comes out clean.

4 Leave to cool in the tin for 10 minutes, then turn out on to a wire rack to cool completely.

5 Meanwhile, make the Marmite butter. Using a hand mixer, whip the butter and Marmite together until light and fluffy.

TO FREEZE THE LOAF
Allow to cool completely and wrap it tightly in foil. Freeze for up to 2 months and defrost before using. Alternatively, cool completely and freeze in slices so that you don't have to defrost the whole loaf – you can toast the slices directly from frozen to eat.

You can store the Marmite butter in an airtight container for up to 2 months.

Cheese, chive and ham hock scones

Warm, savoury scones, fresh from the oven, and spread with a little butter are great for breakfast on the go. Traditional plain scones don't always freeze well, but these are a happy exception. Why not double the recipe and make a couple of batches for the freezer too?

MAKES 2 SCONE ROUNDS

50g butter
300g self-raising flour, plus extra for kneading
180g mature cheddar, finely grated
50g cooked ham hock, finely chopped
small pinch of cayenne pepper
2 tbsp finely chopped chives
2 eggs, beaten
4–5 tbsp milk
salt and black pepper to season

1   Preheat the oven to 200°C/180°C fan/ Gas mark 6 and grease a large baking sheet.

2   Tip the butter and flour into a large mixing bowl. Rub the butter into the flour until it looks like fine breadcrumbs and season well with salt and pepper.

3   Stir in 120g of the grated cheddar, along with the ham hock, cayenne pepper and chopped chives. Add three quarters of the beaten egg and stir with a knife, then gradually add the milk, just until you have a soft, loose dough.

4   Scatter a little flour on to your work surface. Knead the dough until it becomes smooth. Don't be tempted to keep going beyond this or it will become tough.

5   Cut the dough in half, and shape into 2 rounds. Press down gently until each round is about 2cm high.

6   Place the rounds on the greased baking sheet and cut each into 6 triangles, pushing the triangles apart to create a little space between each one. Brush with the rest of the beaten egg and sprinkle the remaining cheddar over the top. Bake for 20–22 minutes until well risen and nicely golden. Serve warm.

TO FREEZE
Allow to cool completely, then wrap the rounds tightly in foil. Freeze for up to 2 months.

TO REHEAT
Preheat the oven to 180°C/160°C fan/Gas mark 4 and place, still wrapped in foil, on a baking tray. Heat for 20–25 minutes until hot.

Perfectly portioned shakshuka

Shakshuka is a vibrantly and energetically flavoured Middle Eastern breakfast dish. There are endless variations of the basic recipe, which is based around eggs poached in a spiced tomato sauce. It's a sunny, colourful and uplifting meal, packed with multi-coloured peppers and warming spices.

This is a hearty version, cooked and served from the same pan, and ideal for sharing at breakfast time with a big group of noisy friends and family. You can make the tomato base in advance and keep it in the fridge for a few days until you need it, or you can freeze it for up to 2 months. Feeds 6 generously, but you can also freeze the sauce in single serving-sized portions.

4 tbsp olive oil
1 onion, finely diced
4 garlic cloves, crushed
2 red peppers, deseeded and diced
2 green peppers, deseeded and diced
2 yellow peppers, deseeded and diced
2 tsp ground cumin
1 tsp smoked paprika
2 tbsp tomato purée
¼ tsp chipotle paste or 2 tbsp harissa paste
3 x 400g tins of chopped tomatoes
1 tsp runny honey or granulated sugar
1 tsp salt, plus extra to season
black pepper to season

TO SERVE
6 eggs
4 tbsp chopped flat-leaf parsley

1 Heat the oil in a large, heavy-bottomed saucepan or sauté pan on a medium heat, add the onion and garlic and gently fry for 8–10 minutes until soft and translucent.

2 Add the peppers, spices, tomato purée, chipotle or harissa paste and cook for 2 minutes.

Pour in the tinned tomatoes and half a tin of water and stir well. Add the honey or sugar, the teaspoon of salt and a generous grind of pepper and bring to a gentle simmer. Partially cover, and simmer very gently for 20 minutes until rich and syrupy. Taste and add more salt and pepper if needed.

3 If you are serving the shakshuka immediately, make 6 dips in the sauce with the back of a spoon and gently break an egg into each one. Cover immediately with a lid and continue simmering gently for a further 6–8 minutes until the eggs are cooked through. Sprinkle with parsley and serve.

TO FREEZE
Allow the tomato sauce to cool completely and freeze in 6 separate portions in bags or freezer-proof containers. Defrost completely before reheating.

Reheat in a saucepan. Heat until piping hot. Turn the heat down to a gentle simmer, then make a well in the sauce and break in an egg. Cover with a lid and cook for 5–6 minutes until the white is cooked and the yolk is still runny. Scatter with chopped parsley and serve.

Wherever or however you eat, lunch needs to fulfil some basic criteria. It should be filling enough to satisfy yet not weigh you down, and if you're on the go, it should be portable too. And above all, it has to taste fabulous.

3 | Batch lunches — at home and on the go

During the week, lunch is often a hasty and practical meal fuelled by necessity rather than desire. But even if it's nothing more than a quick desk sandwich or a bowl of too-hot soup wolfed down before racing out, for most of us it's the first opportunity to stop and breathe. It's a time to draw a line under the morning and fortify ourselves for what is still to come.

That's where batch cooking comes in. If you're a fan of traditional soup and sandwich lunches, you'll be very happy. Soup freezes well and it's not precious about ingredients, so you can throw it together using not much more than a stock cube and whatever you can find in the fridge, adding bulk with meat, veg or grains if you're extra hungry. And discovering you can freeze sandwiches is a revelation for toastie lovers, especially if you're working from home or have a workplace kitchen. Just build yourself a tower of sandwiches and wrap them up tightly for the freezer where they can wait patiently for their moment.

If you prefer your lunches light, making your own hummus is quick, easy and cheap. Shop-bought hummus is popular, but often packed with sugar and salt, so make your own instead, experimenting with new flavours and textures to find your favourites. When you've made a big batch, decant it into small lunch-sized airtight boxes for the fridge and freezer. Add some veggie balls or rolls for dipping. And if you're in need of a more substantial lunch, baked potatoes are a great source of fibre and energy. Baking lots of potatoes at once and stuffing them for the freezer is a good way of making sure you get the most from your oven.

So instead of relying on whatever you can find at the last minute, allocate a little time to fill up your fridge and freezer with these delicious lunch batches and you'll breeze through the week, eating healthy, budget-friendly food with the minimum effort.

The best batch lunches

Gruyère, sun-dried tomato and chilli toasties

Frozen Welsh rarebit crumpet toppers

Basil, sun-dried tomato and goat's cheese spirals

Mushroom, walnut and parsley soup

Kale, leek and bacon soup

Curried smoked fish chowder

Courgette, fennel and dill balls

Stuffed jackets with mushrooms and pancetta

Croque monsieur pies

Heavenly hummus: Caramelised onion, wild garlic, spicy butternut

Poppy seed, mozzarella and ham Bierocks

Gruyère, sun-dried tomato and chilli toasties

Toasted sandwiches are our favourite round-the-clock munchies. With just a few minutes of prep, you can load up the freezer with toasties and never be far from a quick meal. Just remember, the butter goes on the outside of the sandwich!

MAKES 4

butter, softened, for spreading
8 slices of bread
2 tbsp tomato and chilli jam, or ½ tsp finely
    chopped fresh red chilli
150g Gruyère cheese, grated
4 sun-dried tomatoes, finely chopped
½ tbsp finely chopped chives

1 Lay out 4 sheets of cling film on a work surface.

2 Butter each slice of bread on one side, and place 4 of the slices, butter sides downwards, on top of the cling-film sheets.

3 Spread ½ tablespoon of tomato and chilli jam or a sprinkling of fresh chilli on each of these 4 slices.

4 Divide the Gruyère evenly between the 4 slices and scatter the sun-dried tomatoes and chives over the top.

5 Place the 4 remaining slices, butter sides upwards, on the top so you have 4 sandwiches. Wrap each sandwich individually in the cling film.

TO FREEZE
These can be cooked straight from frozen and last in the freezer for up to 2 months.

TO COOK
Remove the cling film and heat a non-stick frying pan over a medium heat. Place the sandwiches in the pan, and cook for 4–5 minutes on each side until crisply golden and the cheese has melted. Press down with a spatula so they cook evenly. You may need to turn the heat down slightly for the second side to prevent that side from cooking too quickly as the pan gets hotter.

ALTERNATIVE HAM, CHEESE AND PICKLE FILLING:
butter, softened, for spreading
8 slices of bread
150g red Leicester cheese, grated
4 slices of ham
2 tbsp tangy pickle

Frozen Welsh rarebit crumpet toppers

This is a delightfully indulgent and freezer-friendly lunch or easy starter that takes a mere 2 minutes to cook. Freezing Welsh rarebit toppings is a clever cooking hack from professional chefs, who usually cut it into loaf-sized slices. Here, it's cut into crumpet-sized circles that can be frozen in layers until needed.

FEEDS 8

300g mature cheddar, grated
50ml double cream
2 tbsp Worcestershire sauce
1 tsp wholegrain mustard
few drops of Tabasco sauce
1 egg yolk
8 crumpets, to serve

1   Line the base and sides of a 20cm x 20cm baking tin with greaseproof paper or a reusable liner.

2   Mix the cheese and cream in a small saucepan and warm gently over a low heat, stirring continuously until the cheese has melted completely. Stir in the Worcestershire sauce, mustard and Tabasco and remove from the heat. Cool for 10 minutes, then add the egg yolk and mix until completely combined.

3   Pour the rarebit mixture into the lined tin and cover with another sheet of greaseproof paper or another liner. Freeze for 40–60 minutes until firm enough to cut.

4   Lift the liner on to a large chopping board and use a round 9cm (or so) pastry cutter or cup rim to cut out crumpet-sized circles of the rarebit mixture.

5   Collect up any trimmings and re-roll them between the greaseproof paper sheets. Cut out more circles and re-roll again until you have 8 rarebit circles.

TO FREEZE
Freeze the circles of rarebit between sheets of greaseproof paper for up to 2 months.

TO COOK
Toast the crumpets on both sides, place a circle of frozen rarebit on top of each crumpet and cook under a medium grill until golden.

Basil, sun-dried tomato and goat's cheese spirals

Everyone loves warm, fresh bread and these summery tear-and-share rolls are ideal for lunch. Serve them with warm soup or stuff them with your favourite sandwich ingredients, but if you are hungry, get in quick as they disappear very fast!

MAKES 8–9 ROLLS

500g strong white bread flour, plus
    extra for dusting
10g salt
10g easy dried yeast
2 tbsp mixed seeds (optional)
pinch of paprika
grinding of black pepper
300ml tepid water
2 tbsp olive oil
5 tbsp sun-dried tomato paste
200g soft goat's cheese, very thinly sliced
bunch of basil, leaves picked
1 egg, beaten

1 Place the flour, salt, yeast and mixed seeds (if using) into a large mixing bowl. Make a well in the centre with a spoon, add a pinch of paprika and a good grinding of black pepper.

2 Mix the warm water with the olive oil and pour it into the well. Slowly stir the water into the flour to create a soft dough. Turn out on to a floured surface and knead until the dough becomes smooth and silky. Add a little more flour if the mixture is very wet.

3 Place the dough in a greased bowl and cover with a tea towel. Leave to rise for 60 minutes until doubled in size.

4 Line a large round baking tin with greaseproof paper or a reusable liner, and preheat the oven to 200°C/180°C fan/Gas mark 6.

5 Turn out the dough on to a floured surface and roll it out into a 25cm x 25cm rectangle.

6 Spread the sun-dried tomato paste evenly across the dough, and scatter goat's cheese slices over the top. Set aside a small handful of basil leaves and tear the rest into small pieces. Sprinkle the torn basil over the cheese.

7 From the longest side of the dough, carefully roll the whole piece into a long log shape. Cut it into 8 or 9 large slices and place these snugly into the baking tin. Cover with greased cling film or a reusable cover and place somewhere warm to prove for 30 minutes.

8 When the spirals have risen nicely, brush the top with beaten egg and bake for 20–25 minutes until golden. Serve immediately, sprinkled with the reserved basil.

TO FREEZE
Allow to cool completely, then wrap in foil and place in the freezer. Freeze for up to 2 months.

TO REHEAT FROM FROZEN
Heat the oven to 180°C/160°C fan/Gas mark 4, loosen the foil slightly and warm through for 20–25 minutes until piping hot. Alternatively, allow to defrost completely, remove from the foil and microwave for 2–3 minutes or until warmed through.

Mushroom, walnut and parsley soup

Mushroom soup is always good, but it comes in especially handy when there is a sad box of past-their-best fungi at the bottom of the fridge. Soup is the answer, and walnuts bring a rich, nutty crunchiness that balances the creamy mushrooms.

FEEDS 4–6

90g butter
20g flat-leaf parsley, stalks finely chopped
    and leaves chopped
2 onions, finely chopped
750g mushrooms (any), sliced
½ tsp salt, plus extra to season
glug of white wine or sherry (optional)
1 litre chicken stock
80g walnuts, chopped
200ml single cream
black pepper to season
croutons, to serve

1 Melt the butter in a heavy-based saucepan on a medium heat and add the parsley stalks, half of the chopped parsley leaves and the chopped onions. Fry gently for 6–8 minutes until the onions are softened but not browned. Add the sliced mushrooms and the ½ teaspoon of salt, then turn up the heat and fry quickly for 10 minutes, stirring continuously, until the mushrooms have softened and any released liquid has evaporated. If you are using wine or sherry, pour it in now and stir until it evaporates.

2 Add the stock and bring to the boil. Turn the heat down and simmer gently for 20 minutes, then add the chopped walnuts and purée with a stick blender until smooth. Taste the soup and add pepper and extra salt to season if required.

3 If you are serving the soup immediately, stir in the cream and heat through very gently without boiling. Sprinkle with the remaining chopped parsley leaves and top with the croutons to serve.

TO FREEZE
Do not add the cream to the blended soup. Cool the soup completely, then seal in an airtight container and freeze for up to 2 months. Defrost completely, then stir in the cream and warm slowly and gently without boiling.

Kale, leek and bacon soup

This is probably the most frequently requested lunch in our house. It's not only healthy and tasty, it's great for recycling as you can happily throw in any old veggies that need using up. It's also good for using up leftover cooked bacon if you've made too much for breakfast (just stir it in when the soup is cooked).

FEEDS 4

1 tsp olive oil
4 slices of smoked streaky bacon, finely sliced
    (or use leftover cooked bacon)
15g butter
1 tsp thyme leaves
2 leeks, trimmed and cut into thin coins
2 carrots, peeled, quartered lengthways and
    finely chopped
2 celery sticks, finely chopped
20g flat-leaf parsley, leaves and stalks chopped
    separately
50g kale, finely sliced
1 litre chicken or vegetable stock
1 large potato, washed, skin left on, chopped
    into 1cm cubes
salt and black pepper to season

1   If you're using uncooked bacon, heat the oil in a large saucepan on a medium heat, then increase the heat to high and fry the bacon for 3–4 minutes until golden. Turn down the heat and add the butter, thyme, leeks, carrots, celery, parsley stalks and kale and sauté for 12–15 minutes until soft.

2   Add the stock and cubed potato and bring to the boil, then turn down the heat and simmer for 10–12 minutes until the potato is cooked through.

3   If you are using cooked bacon, add it to the soup now and cook for another 2–3 minutes to warm through.

4   Season to taste with salt and pepper, sprinkle with chopped parsley and serve.

TO FREEZE
Allow to cool completely and freeze (in portions, if you like) for up to 2 months. Defrost and reheat slowly until piping hot.

Curried smoked fish chowder

This is a rich and substantial soup, with plenty of heft and flavour. Topped with a poached egg, it makes a surprisingly substantial supper. It will keep for a few days in the fridge.

FEEDS 4

1 tbsp olive oil
1 celery stick, finely chopped
1 onion, finely chopped
1 leek, finely chopped
1 carrot, peeled and grated
½ tsp medium curry powder
½ tsp ground cumin
½ tsp ground coriander
½ tsp turmeric
1 tbsp plain flour
500ml chicken stock
1 potato, washed and cut into 1cm cubes
300g skinless smoked haddock, chopped into 3cm chunks
3 tbsp single cream
1 x 150g tin of sweetcorn, drained
salt and black pepper to season
1 tbsp chopped chives, to serve

1 Heat the oil in a heavy-bottomed pan on a medium heat and add the chopped celery, onion and leek and the grated carrot. Cover and cook gently for about 10–15 minutes until the vegetables are soft. Tip in the spices and cook for another 2 minutes until fragrant.

2 Sprinkle the flour over the vegetables and stir well, then gradually pour in the chicken stock. Add the diced potato and bring to the boil. Turn down the heat and allow the mixture to simmer gently for 6–8 minutes until the sauce has thickened and the potatoes are cooked through.

3 Add the haddock and simmer for 3–4 minutes until cooked, stirring gently. Stir in the cream and sweetcorn, warm through, then season with salt and pepper. Sprinkle with the chives to serve.

MAKE AHEAD
If not eating immediately, allow to cool completely, then refrigerate. To reheat, place in a saucepan and heat very gently until warmed through, but do not allow to boil.

Courgette, fennel and dill balls

These little green balls are a great vegetarian alternative to meatballs. They were a quick fix when newly vegetarian friends came for supper and the fridge yielded just a few onions and a fennel bulb, but they became a family favourite very fast. You can freeze them too.

MAKES 25–30 BALLS – ENOUGH TO FEED 6

600g courgettes, trimmed and coarsely grated
1 tsp salt, plus extra to season
20g butter
1 tbsp olive oil
1 small fennel bulb, trimmed and finely chopped, fronds reserved
2 garlic cloves, crushed
140g feta cheese, crumbled
3 tbsp chopped dill
generous grinding of black pepper, plus extra to season
60g gram or plain flour
vegetable oil, for frying
150g natural yoghurt

1 Place the grated courgettes in a colander and toss with the salt. Place over a bowl or sink and leave for 30 minutes to drain.

2 While the courgettes are salting, heat the butter and oil in a frying pan on a medium–high heat and fry the fennel and garlic for 10 minutes until softened but not browned. Set aside to cool slightly.

3 Tip the grated courgettes into the centre of a clean tea towel and gather the 4 corners together. Twist them firmly to squeeze the excess liquid out of the courgettes. Continue until no more liquid comes out of the bottom of the tea towel.

4 Place the courgettes, fennel mixture, feta cheese and 2 tablespoons of the chopped dill into a large bowl. Add a generous grinding of black pepper and the flour and mix well.

5 With damp hands, roll the courgette mixture into balls, each about the size of a small walnut, and place them on a baking tray lined with greaseproof paper. Chill for 30–60 minutes. (See freezer notes now if you intend to freeze.)

6 To cook the balls, pour 2 tablespoons of vegetable oil into a non-stick frying pan over a medium–high heat. When the oil is hot, place 6–8 balls into the pan and fry until they are golden brown on all sides. Drain on kitchen paper and keep warm. Continue until all the balls are cooked.

7 Mix the yoghurt with the remaining chopped dill and season with salt and pepper.

8 Sprinkle the courgette balls with the reserved fennel fronds and serve with the yoghurt and dill dip alongside.

TO FREEZE
Place the baking tray of uncooked balls, uncovered, in the freezer for 40 minutes. When they are firm enough to stack without squashing, place into an airtight bag or box, between layers of greaseproof paper, and freeze for up to 2 months. Cook from frozen as above until cooked through.

Stuffed jackets with mushrooms and pancetta

Who knew that baked potatoes froze so well? Well, they do, and as they are best made in the oven, rather than the microwave, it makes sense to cook a big batch and have some to hand for busy, hungry days. This recipe uses everyday mushrooms, but if you're lucky enough to come across edible wild mushrooms, use them instead.

FEEDS 4

4 large baking potatoes
2 tsp olive oil, plus extra for frying
50g butter
300g any medium-sized mushrooms, sliced
160g pancetta or streaky bacon, sliced into
    small pieces
2 tbsp chopped chives, plus extra to serve
50g Parmesan or mature cheddar, finely grated
4 tbsp milk
Maldon salt and black pepper

1   Preheat the oven to 200°C/180°C fan/ Gas mark 6.

2   Prick the potatoes a few times with a fork then rub a little olive oil over the skins. Place them on a roasting tray and scatter with a teaspoon of salt.

3   Bake for 60–90 minutes until the skins are crisp and the potatoes are cooked through. Set aside for 15 minutes until cool enough to handle.

4   While the potatoes are cooking, melt the butter in a frying pan on a medium–high heat, add a good pinch of salt and fry the mushrooms for 8–10 minutes until golden brown. Remove with a slotted spoon and set aside in a mixing bowl. Add the pancetta or bacon pieces to the

pan and fry quickly until crispy all over, adding a little olive oil if needed. Tip into the mushroom mixture, add the chopped chives and grated cheese and stir well.

5   Cut the potatoes in half lengthways and, without breaking the skins, carefully scoop out the flesh and mash it in a bowl together with the milk. Stir the mashed potato into the mushrooms and bacon and season to taste. Divide the mixture equally between the potato halves. (See freezer notes now if you intend to freeze.)

6   If you're eating straight away, place in the oven for 15–20 minutes until golden on top and warmed through.

TO FREEZE
Cool the filled (but not re-baked) potatoes completely, then place in an airtight container or foil freezer container and freeze for up to 2 months. To cook from frozen, loosely cover with foil and place in the oven at 200°C/180°C fan/Gas mark 6 for 30–35 minutes until golden brown and warmed through.

Croque monsieur pies

These little treats are basically croque monsieurs in a handy mini pie. They are great for wrapping in foil and eating warm on the go, or served up hot for a snack or light lunch. If you already have white sauce (see p.18) in the fridge or freezer, you can use it to replace the butter, flour and milk. Just bring it to the simmer before adding the next ingredients.

MAKES 8

30g butter
30g plain flour
200ml milk
½ tsp mustard powder
generous pinch of paprika
2 x 375g sheets of ready-rolled puff pastry
1 egg, beaten
50g mature cheddar, grated
150g Comté or Gruyère cheese, grated
130g finely sliced ham
salt and black pepper to season

1 Melt the butter in a small saucepan and stir in the flour to form a golden paste. Gradually whisk in the milk and, as the sauce thickens, add the mustard powder and paprika and season generously with salt and pepper. Cook for another 3–4 minutes until thick and smooth, then cover and set aside to cool.

2 If you are cooking the pies straight away, preheat the oven to 200°C/180°C fan/Gas mark 6 and grease 2 large baking sheets.

3 Unroll the pastry sheets on to 2 large sheets of greaseproof paper. Place a piece of greaseproof paper over 1 pastry sheet and, using a rolling pin, roll the sheet 2cm larger (you'll use this sheet for the pie lids).

4 Cut each sheet of puff pastry into 8 equal-sized pieces.

5 Brush the edges of the 8 smaller pieces with beaten egg. Spread a spoonful of sauce in the centre of each piece, leaving a 1cm border.

6 Combine the cheeses in a bowl. Sprinkle some cheese over the sauce and within the border, and add a layer of ham (also to fit within the border). Repeat with another layer of sauce, cheese and ham, then a final layer of cheese, and finish with a layer of sauce on the top.

7 Place the remaining 8 larger squares of pastry over the top and gently press around the edges with the tines of a fork. Trim any scraggly bits with a sharp knife and use the trimmings to decorate the pies with shapes or letters. Make a slit in the top of each pie to let the steam out. (See freezer notes now if you intend to freeze.)

8 To cook straight away, brush the pies with beaten egg and bake for 30–35 minutes until golden.

TO FREEZE
Wrap the uncooked pies in foil and freeze for up to 2 months. To cook from frozen, remove the foil, brush the pies with beaten egg and cook at 200°C/180°C fan/Gas mark 6 for 40–45 minutes.

Heavenly hummus: caramelised onion, wild garlic, spicy butternut

I think hummus is addictive, whether it's the much-loved basic variety or a more adventurous creation. Homemade hummus is not only easy to make, it's better for you, and guess what? You can freeze it too. So here's a trio of colourful, vibrant hummuses that, if you're anything like me, will keep your hummus habit satisfied.

CARAMELISED ONION HUMMUS

FOR THE CARAMELISED ONIONS

2 small red onions, very finely sliced
5 tbsp balsamic vinegar
2 tbsp runny honey
1½ tbsp olive oil

FOR THE HUMMUS

2 x 400g tins of chickpeas, drained and rinsed
2 tbsp tahini paste
2 tbsp lemon juice
2 garlic cloves, crushed
100ml olive oil, plus extra for drizzling
salt and black pepper to season

Place all the caramelised onion ingredients in a small saucepan and bring to the boil. Turn the heat down as low as possible, then cover and simmer for 25–30 minutes, stirring occasionally, until the mixture is caramelised. Set aside to cool for 10 minutes.

To make the hummus, place the chickpeas, tahini, lemon juice, garlic and olive oil in a food processor and blitz until smooth. Set aside 3 tablespoons of caramelised onion, then tip the rest into the food processor. Blitz again until smooth, adding a little cold water if the hummus is too stiff. Taste and add salt and pepper. Drizzle with olive oil, and spoon the reserved onions on the top before serving.

WILD GARLIC HUMMUS

1 x 400g tin of chickpeas, drained and rinsed
20g wild garlic leaves, roughly chopped
3 tbsp tahini paste
juice of 1 lemon
½ tbsp olive oil, plus extra if necessary
    and for drizzling
½ tsp Maldon salt
black pepper to season

Put the chickpeas, wild garlic, tahini and lemon juice into a food processor and blitz to a paste. While the motor is still running add 50ml of water and the oil into the feeder tube. Process until very smooth, adding a little more oil if needed. Add the salt and some pepper to taste and drizzle with olive oil.

SPICY BUTTERNUT HUMMUS

500g butternut squash (peeled, deseeded and cubed weight)

4 garlic cloves, unpeeled

5 tbsp olive oil, plus extra for drizzling

2 x 400g tins of chickpeas, drained and rinsed

1 tsp ground cumin

½ tsp cayenne pepper

1 tbsp lemon juice

2 tbsp tahini paste

1 red chilli, deseeded and finely chopped

salt and black pepper to season

1   Heat the oven to 200°C/180°C fan/Gas mark 6.

2   Toss the butternut squash cubes and garlic in 2 tablespoons of the olive oil, then season with salt and pepper and roast for 40–45 minutes, turning occasionally until caramelised around the edges.

3   Place the remaining oil and ingredients into a food processor and blitz until very smooth.

4   Squeeze the roasted garlic out of its peel into the processor, add the cooked butternut and blitz again, pouring in a little cold water if needed to loosen. Add salt and pepper to taste and drizzle with olive oil.

TO FREEZE THE HUMMUS

Drizzle with olive oil and place in airtight containers for up to 2 months. Defrost and stir before eating.

Poppy seed, mozzarella and ham Bierocks

Every country has some form of filled savoury roll or sandwich, from Cornish pasties and Argentinian empanadas to Italian paninis. These little filled rolls are German, and are traditionally filled with minced meat and cabbage, but my lighter ham, cheese and spinach version is ideal for a simple lunch or food on the go.

MAKES 20

300ml lukewarm water
1 tbsp caster sugar
7g easy dried yeast
1 tbsp olive oil, plus extra for greasing
500g plain flour, plus extra for dusting
2 tsp salt
1 tbsp poppy seeds
2 tbsp chopped flat-leaf parsley
8 slices of medium-sliced ham, chopped
    into 1cm pieces
250g mozzarella, diced
2 small handfuls of baby spinach,
    finely chopped
50g butter, melted
1–2 tsp sesame seeds
black pepper to season

1   To make the dough, pour the lukewarm water into a mixing jug and stir in the sugar and yeast. Leave to bubble a little for 10 minutes, then stir in the tablespoon of olive oil.

2   Mix the flour, salt, poppy seeds and parsley together in a large mixing bowl and make a dip in the centre. Pour the water and yeast mixture into the dip and slowly mix into the flour. It will be very sticky at first but keep stirring until it starts to come together. When you can form a soft, raggedy ball of dough, tip it out on to a floured surface and knead for 10 minutes until it's smooth and springy. Clean the mixing bowl and grease with a little oil, then place the dough inside. Cover with greased cling film or a reusable lid and place somewhere warm to rise for 40–50 minutes, until about doubled in size.

3   Line 2 large baking trays with greaseproof paper or reusable liners.

4   Split the dough into 20 pieces. On a floured surface, roll out each piece into a small saucer-sized circle. Pile the ham, mozzarella and spinach equally into the centre of each circle. Season well with salt and pepper, then paint the edge of each circle with water.

5 Bring the edges of each dough circle together over the filling and press with your fingers to seal. Turn over each roll so that the seam is underneath. As you complete each roll, place it on the lined baking tray. Cover with greased cling film and leave to rise somewhere warm for 30 minutes.

6 Heat the oven to 180°C/160°C fan/Gas mark 4.

7 Brush the rolls with melted butter, sprinkle with sesame seeds and bake for 25–30 minutes until puffy and golden. Remove from the oven and place on a cooling rack. Brush again with melted butter and serve warm.

TO FREEZE THE COOKED BIEROCKS
Allow to cool completely, then place them in an airtight box or bag between layers of greaseproof paper or reusable liners. Freeze for up to 2 months. To reheat, place the buns on a greased baking sheet and heat through at 180°C/160°C fan/Gas mark 4 for 15–20 minutes.

Weekdays are where batch meals really come into their own, feeding and fuelling our lives with make-ahead dishes and standby suppers that cheer and soothe at the end of a long day.

4 | Everyday feasts — the busy cook's TV dinners

A workday supper can and should be as delicious as a leisurely dinner at the weekend, but when you're exhausted after a long day there's often precious little time or energy to cook a complicated supper.

Batch cooking is the answer, but it's all too easy to use the same recipes every time. There's nothing wrong with a good bolognese, but as the weeks and months roll past, that mince recipe can get a little dull. Which means that instead of a fragrant, delicious meal to reward yourself for all your hard work during the day, you find yourself uninspired and suddenly not as hungry as you thought.

So the next time you're setting aside precious time for a batch cook, make it an adventurous one! This chapter is packed with great new recipes to keep your week rolling tastily along, such as the one-pot chicken casserole and slow-cooked lamb shanks that are easily repurposed into hearty sauces, quick beef stroganoff freezer pies, savoury broccoli pancakes and punchy multi-tasking meatballs that are divine for supper, but also make great snacks or starters. The recipes all feed at least four and are easily multiplied for bigger batches.

Some dishes are ideal for freezing, whilst others keep perfectly for a few days in the fridge, but without exception, they will all deliver a feast to cheer the soul when you most need it.

The best batch everyday feasts

Tarragon, fennel and cider one-pot chicken

Revision-friendly chicken and mustard pie

Broccoli, bacon and blue cheese pancakes

Quick turkey and apple meatballs

Pork, coriander and miso meatballs

Big oven-baked broad bean and pancetta risotto

Chorizo, fennel and chickpea tagine

Slow-cooked Moroccan lamb shanks

Merguez sausage and lentil stew

Speedy beef stroganoff pies with a crunchy herb topping

One-pot quick fish curry with noodles and pak choi

Frozen honey-soy salmon parcels

Tarragon, fennel and cider one-pot chicken

This wonderful dish tastes as if you've been slaving away in the kitchen for hours, when in reality all you've done is fry a few veggies and thrown everything into a pot. The combination of fresh, lemony tarragon with warm mustard undertones brings real vigour to a simple roast chicken dish. You can repurpose the leftover chicken carcass to make a delicious stock.

FEEDS 4–6

knob of butter
1 tbsp olive oil, plus more for oiling
2 garlic cloves, crushed
1 fennel bulb, cored, halved and finely sliced,
    trimmings saved
1 Spanish onion, finely sliced
300g mushrooms (any type), thickly sliced
1 tbsp chopped tarragon leaves,
    plus extra to serve
330ml cider
1.6–1.8kg (large) chicken
2 tbsp wholegrain mustard
4 tbsp single cream
salt and black pepper to season

1   Preheat the oven to 180°C/160°C fan/ Gas mark 4.

2   Heat the butter and oil together in a flameproof casserole. Add the garlic, fennel, onion, mushrooms and chopped tarragon. Cook for 10–12 minutes until the vegetables have softened. Pour in the cider and bring to the boil.

3   Oil the chicken and season well with salt and pepper. Place the chicken on top of the vegetables and roast, covered, for 45 minutes. Remove the lid, baste and roast uncovered for a further 25–35 minutes, basting occasionally, until the skin is crispy and the chicken is cooked through.

4   Remove the chicken from the casserole and keep warm.

5   Put the casserole on the hob and bring the liquid to the boil. Cook for 8–10 minutes until reduced by half, then turn the heat right down and add the mustard and cream and gently warm without boiling. Taste the sauce and add more seasoning if needed. Pour the sauce with all its bits into a jug, sprinkle the chicken with extra tarragon leaves and serve.

LEFTOVERS

If any meat is left on the chicken, strip it from the bones and place in an airtight container with leftover sauce. This will keep in the fridge for 2 days. Reheat it gently until piping hot (but without boiling) and serve with couscous or rice.

Revision-friendly chicken and mustard pie

I created this recipe during my daughter's GCSE season to turn grim maths revision into something altogether more palatable. It's a soothing, velvety pie that will fuel and sustain even the most hard-working diners, and you can reheat any leftovers to enjoy another day. In theory, the pastry has more than enough carbs to keep everyone happy, but there is nothing like buttery mashed potato to mop up the juices of a perfect pie. Just saying. Makes 1 large pie or 4 small ones.

FEEDS 4

40g butter
1 tbsp olive oil
1 onion, finely chopped
20g flat-leaf parsley, stalks and leaves separated
    and finely chopped
6 carrots, peeled and sliced into thin rounds
1kg skinless, boneless chicken thighs, each cut
    into 4–6 pieces
4 tbsp plain flour
400ml chicken stock
1½ tbsp wholegrain mustard
2 tbsp single cream
140g frozen peas
100g tinned sweetcorn, drained
1 sheet of ready-rolled puff pastry
1 egg, beaten
salt and black pepper to season
mashed potato, to serve

1 Heat the butter and oil together in a large heavy-based saucepan. Add the chopped onion and parsley stalks and cook for 8–10 minutes until soft.

2 Add the carrots and chicken and cook for 15 minutes, stirring regularly, until the chicken is lightly cooked. Add the flour and stir well before pouring in the chicken stock. Bring everything to a simmer and cook for another 10 minutes. Season well, and stir in the mustard, cream, chopped parsley leaves, peas and sweetcorn.

3 Heat the oven to 200°C/180°C fan/Gas mark 6 and grease a deep ovenproof dish a little smaller than your puff pastry sheet (or grease 4 small pie dishes). Pour in the filling (dividing it equally if making individual pies). (See freezer notes now if you intend to freeze.)

4 Brush the rim of the dish (or dishes) with a little beaten egg. Drape the puff pastry over the top of the dish so it is overhanging slightly at each end. (Or, divide the pastry into equal-sized pieces and do the same for each individual pie.)

5 Trim the edges and save the trimmings. Press the tines of a fork evenly around the rim to seal the pastry lid(s).

6 For extra marks, cut out the mathematical symbol for Pi from the pastry trimmings and place on top. Make a slit in the top of the pie(s) to allow the steam to escape.

7 If you are baking straight away, brush with the remaining beaten egg and place in the preheated oven for 40–45 minutes until the top is golden brown and the filling is piping hot.

TO FREEZE

Allow the filling to cool completely before covering with the pastry lids. Wrap in foil and freeze for up to 1 month. To bake a large pie from frozen, heat the oven to 180°C/160°C fan/Gas mark 4 and bake for 60–70 minutes until the top is golden brown and the filling is piping hot.

If you have made 4 smaller pies, cook from frozen for 35–45 minutes.

Broccoli, bacon and blue cheese pancakes

Stuffed pancakes do feel a bit retro, probably because of the popular TV-dinner version of them in the 1980s. But pancakes make a brilliant base for savoury fillings, and because they freeze so well, they're ideal for batch cooking. All you need to do is to whip them out of the freezer and fill them with anything from ham and cheese to curried chickpeas. Here, the filling is a classic combination of broccoli, bacon and blue cheese. So next time you're making pancakes for breakfast, flip an extra batch in preparation. If you have white sauce ready made (see p.18), place 400ml in a saucepan, heat until piping hot, then stir in the cheese and season with black pepper. The whole recipe makes 8 filled pancakes, to feed 4.

FOR THE PANCAKE BATTER
120g plain flour
¼ tsp salt
1 egg
300ml milk
butter, for frying and greasing
chopped chives, to serve

FOR THE SAUCE
25g butter
25g plain flour
350ml milk
100g blue cheese, crumbled
black pepper to season

FOR THE FILLING
400g long stem broccoli, trimmed
8 slices of streaky bacon, cooked and crumbled

1 First, make the pancake batter. Sift the flour and salt into a small bowl and whisk in the egg. Little by little, add the milk, whisking in between each addition, until you have a smooth batter. Chill for 30 minutes while you prepare the sauce.

2 To make the sauce, melt the butter in a small saucepan and add the flour, stirring until you have a paste. Add the milk a little at a time, stirring continuously, until the sauce thickens. Bring to the boil and stir for 2 minutes to get rid of any persistent lumps, then turn off the heat. Set aside 2 tablespoons of blue cheese, and stir the rest into the sauce. Season with black pepper, then cover and set aside.

3 Start the filling. Boil the broccoli in a large saucepan of salted water for 3 minutes, then drain and set aside.

4   To cook the pancakes, heat a small non-stick frying pan over a medium heat. Add a knob of butter, swirling it around to cover the base of the pan. When it's hot, add a ladleful of batter to the pan and rotate it so that the batter covers the base. Cook until the edges start to crinkle, then check to see if the pancake is lightly golden underneath. When it is, flip it over and cook the other side. When both sides are golden, transfer the pancake to a plate and keep warm. Repeat with the remaining batter, melting a little more butter in the pan between each pancake. You should get 8 equal-sized pancakes altogether. (See freezer notes now if you intend to freeze.)

5   Preheat the oven to 190°C/170°C fan/ Gas mark 5 and grease a 25cm x 25cm shallow ovenproof dish.

6   When the pancakes are ready, place an equal number of the broccoli stems in the centre of each one. Sprinkle the bacon over the top and top with a spoonful of sauce. Roll up the pancakes and place them side by side in the greased dish. Pour over the remaining sauce and sprinkle with the reserved blue cheese. Bake for 15–20 minutes until hot and bubbling. Serve topped with chopped chives.

TO FREEZE THE PANCAKES

Place them between layers of greaseproof paper or reusable liners and slide them into an airtight container. Freeze for up to 2 months. Defrost before filling and cooking as directed in the method.

Quick turkey and apple meatballs

Turkey mince makes a moist, light and budget-friendly alternative to beef and lamb meatballs, and here it's gently sweetened with grated apple. The meatballs are great served with tangy chutney or added to a simple tomato pasta sauce. This recipe makes a whopping 80ish meatballs, but they are obligingly freezable if you can't eat them all at once.

FEEDS 6—8

1kg turkey thigh mince
2 eating apples, peeled, cored and finely grated
6 spring onions, very finely chopped
100g fresh, dried or frozen breadcrumbs
2 tbsp finely chopped flat-leaf parsley leaves
    (use the stalks in a soup base or tomato sauce)
80g mature cheddar, finely grated
2 eggs, beaten
2 tbsp tomato ketchup
¼ tsp paprika
olive oil, for cooking
salt and black pepper to season
chutney or onion marmalade, to serve

1   Mix all the ingredients together in a large mixing bowl and season generously. Take a small walnut-sized amount of mixture and gently roll it into a ball. Place on a sheet of greaseproof paper or a reusable liner set on a large baking tray. Repeat until the mixture is finished. You should have about 80 meatballs. Cover and refrigerate for 1 hour to allow the meatballs to firm up. (See freezer notes now if you intend to freeze.)

2   To cook, heat a non-stick frying pan over a medium heat and pour in a good glug of oil. When it's hot, cook the meatballs in small batches, rolling them over every 3–4 minutes or so as each side browns. Keep the cooked meatballs warm while you cook the rest.

TO FREEZE
Place the uncooked meatballs on a baking tray in the freezer for 1 hour until they are firm enough to hold their shape. Tip into an airtight bag and freeze for up to 1 month. To use, shake the meatballs out on to a baking tray in a single layer and defrost completely before cooking as in the recipe.

Pork, coriander and miso meatballs

Miso is a joyous thing. Here it turns a seemingly straightforward recipe, made with everyday pork mince, into seriously punchy power balls. These make great snacks dipped into a citrusy soy or chilli sauce, but they are also divine dropped into a simple chicken stock with fresh noodles (they will take 2–3 minutes to warm through in a simmering stock). Double up the recipe to make a bigger batch.

FEEDS 4

6 tbsp finely chopped coriander leaves
4 spring onions, finely chopped
2 garlic cloves, crushed
2 tbsp finely grated fresh ginger
2 tbsp light or dark miso paste
1 tbsp light soy sauce, plus extra for dipping
finely grated zest and juice of 1 lime
500g pork mince
4 tbsp vegetable oil, for cooking
black pepper to season

1 Put the coriander, spring onions, garlic, ginger and miso paste into a large bowl and mix together well.

2 Add the soy sauce, lime zest (reserving the juice) and pork mince and a generous grinding of black pepper.

3 Using your hands, mix everything together. Divide the mince into 4 equal piles. Using damp hands, roll 6 equal-sized meatballs from each pile.

4 If you are eating the meatballs straight away, cover and refrigerate for 30 minutes to firm up. (See freezer notes now if you intend to freeze.)

5 When you are ready to cook, heat 2 tablespoons of oil in a large frying pan on a medium–high heat. Cook the meatballs in batches, until they are nicely browned all over, then turn the heat down for 5–6 minutes, until they are cooked through. Keep the cooked meatballs warm while you cook the remaining batches.

6 To serve, mix together the soy sauce with the lime juice and taste, adding a little more lime juice or soy if needed.

TO FREEZE
Place the uncooked meatballs on a baking tray and freeze for 1 hour until they are firm enough to hold their shape. Tip into an airtight bag and freeze for up to 1 month. Shake the meatballs out on to a baking tray in a single layer and defrost completely. Then cook as directed in the recipe.

Big oven-baked broad bean and pancetta risotto

It's easy to be put off risotto when you're busy, which is why the oven-baked version is a gift for the time-poor cook. Apart from a few minutes frying the ingredients and getting the stock up to speed, the oven does all the hard work. Podding the broad beans means you can just enjoy the sweet, emerald-green centres without their chewy grey jackets. This is a substantial risotto and leftovers reheat beautifully.

FEEDS 6

1 tbsp olive oil
8 slices of pancetta, chopped into 1cm pieces
50g butter
1 large onion, finely chopped
2 celery sticks, finely chopped
2 garlic cloves, finely chopped
400g Arborio rice
60ml white wine
800ml hot chicken stock
300g frozen broad beans
60g Parmesan, grated
finely grated zest and juice of 1 lemon
2 tbsp chopped dill
salt and black pepper to season

1 Preheat the oven to 170°C/150°C fan/ Gas mark 3.

2 Heat the oil in a large, shallow, ovenproof casserole dish and quickly fry the pancetta until lightly golden. Remove with a slotted spoon and set aside.

3 Add the butter, onion, celery and garlic to the pan and cook for 8–10 minutes to soften. Tip in the rice, stir, and cook for 2 minutes until the grains are slickly coated with butter and oil.

4 Add the wine and cook quickly until it disappears. Pour in the hot stock and bring to the boil. Place a tight-fitting lid on the casserole (or cover tightly with foil) and bake in the oven for 25–30 minutes, until the stock is absorbed and the rice is cooked.

5 While the rice is cooking, bring a pan of salted water to the boil and cook the broad beans for 2–3 minutes until just cooked. Drain and place in cold water until cool enough to handle, then remove and discard the grey outer pods.

6 When the risotto is ready, stir through the beans, pancetta, Parmesan, lemon zest and 1 tablespoon of lemon juice and warm through. Taste and add more lemon juice, salt and pepper if desired, then mix in the chopped fresh dill and serve.

TO FREEZE

Quickly cool completely, then transfer to an airtight container and freeze for up to 1 month. To cook, defrost from frozen before gently reheating until piping hot. To reheat from frozen, place in a shallow ovenproof dish, cover and cook at 180°C/160°C fan/Gas mark 4 for 20 minutes. Stir, re-cover and cook for 20–25 minutes until piping hot.

Chorizo, fennel and chickpea tagine

Even just a little chorizo brings a rich, smoky flavour to any recipe, and here it's combined with chickpeas and fennel to make a meaty dish with North African flavours. Serve with couscous, flat breads or just in a bowl with a big spoon.

FEEDS 6

1 tbsp olive oil
200g spicy chorizo, halved lengthways
    and thinly sliced
2 fennel bulbs, trimmed and thinly sliced,
    fronds reserved
1 large onion, halved and thinly sliced
2 garlic cloves, crushed
½ tsp smoked paprika
1 tbsp harissa paste
2 x 400g tins of chopped tomatoes
2 tsp runny honey
2 x 400g tins of chickpeas, drained and rinsed
4 handfuls of baby spinach
finely grated zest of 1 lemon
salt and black pepper to season
couscous or flat breads, to serve

1   Heat the oil in a large sauté pan on a medium–high heat and add the sliced chorizo. Cook quickly until slightly crispy, then transfer the chorizo to a side plate using a slotted spoon, leaving the reddish oil in the pan.

2   Turn the heat down and add the fennel, onion, garlic and smoked paprika and sauté for 10–15 minutes until the onion is soft, translucent and starting to turn golden around the edges.

3   Stir in the harissa and a good pinch of salt, and then pour in the tinned tomatoes and a tinful of water. Add the cooked chorizo and the honey, then stir well and bring to the boil. Turn the heat down and simmer for 20–25 minutes until the sauce is thick and syrupy.

4   Add the chickpeas and warm through, then season with salt and pepper.

5   Just before serving, stir the baby spinach through until it wilts, add the lemon zest and scatter over the reserved fennel fronds.

TO FREEZE
Allow the tagine to cool completely then transfer to an airtight container. Freeze for up to 1 month and defrost fully before reheating.

Slow-cooked Moroccan lamb shanks

This is a luxurious, slow-cooked stew, in which the lamb melts off the bone into a rich sauce infused with aromatic spices. Serve with rice or couscous to soak up the veggie-packed sauce. You can freeze any leftovers to eat as a stew or use them to make a soup base. Lamb shanks do vary in size, so this stew feeds 4–6.

½ tsp cayenne pepper
1 tbsp paprika
1 tbsp ground ginger
2 tsp turmeric
1 tsp ground cinnamon
1 tbsp plain flour
4 large lamb shanks
2 tbsp olive oil
2 red onions, finely chopped
2 large carrots, finely chopped
2 celery sticks, finely chopped
2 leeks, finely chopped
3 garlic cloves, crushed
2 x 400g tins of chopped tomatoes
500ml lamb stock
90g dried apricots, chopped
50g flaked almonds, toasted
½ tsp salt, plus extra to season
finely grated zest and juice of 1 lemon
black pepper to season
handful of coriander leaves, to serve
rice or couscous, cooked, to serve

1   Preheat the oven to 180°C/160°C fan/ Gas mark 4.

2   Mix the cayenne, paprika, ginger, turmeric and cinnamon together.

3   Place the flour in a large mixing bowl and stir in half of the mixed spices. Toss the lamb shanks in the spiced flour until dusted all over.

4   Heat 1 tablespoon of oil in a large ovenproof casserole and brown the lamb shanks all over. Remove the shanks to a plate and keep warm.

5   Add the remaining olive oil to the casserole, along with the onions, carrots, celery, leeks and garlic. Cook gently for 10 minutes until soft, then turn up the heat and stir in the remaining mixed spices.

6   Cook for another 3 minutes, then add the tomatoes, stock, apricots, half the flaked almonds, and all the lamb shanks. Stir in ½ teaspoon of salt and season with plenty of black pepper. Bring to the boil, then cover with a tight-fitting lid and transfer to the oven. Cook for 90 minutes, then remove the lid, stir and cook for another 30–40 minutes until the meat is meltingly soft and falling off the bone.

7   When you're ready to eat, skim off any oil and season with salt and pepper to taste. Stir in the lemon zest and juice, and sprinkle with the reserved flaked almonds and the coriander.

LEFTOVERS

Remove any extra meat from the bone and place in an airtight container with any remaining sauce. Allow to cool completely before storing in the fridge for up to 2 days or in the freezer for up to 1 month. Reheat gently.

Merguez sausage and lentil stew

Merguez are long, thin sausages made with lamb or beef and flavoured with North African spices. This is a heartening and filling one-pot supper that you make on the hob. If you can't find merguez sausages, this recipe works just as well with any spicy sausage.

FEEDS 6

1 tbsp olive oil
12 merguez sausages (about 600g)
1 large carrot, peeled and finely chopped
2 red onions, finely chopped
1 red chilli, deseeded and finely chopped
1 red pepper, deseeded and sliced
1 orange pepper, deseeded and sliced
400g dark green or Puy lentils
1 litre vegetable stock
1 x 400g tin of chopped tomatoes
salt and black pepper to season
flat-leaf parsley, chopped, to serve

1   Heat the oil in a large flameproof casserole or heavy-based saucepan on a medium heat and cook the sausages for 10–12 minutes until browned on all sides. Remove with a slotted spatula and set aside.

2   Turn the heat down and add the carrot, onions and chilli and cook gently for 6–8 minutes until the vegetables have softened. Add all the sliced peppers and cook for another 4 minutes, to soften. Finally, add the lentils, vegetable stock and tomatoes and return the sausages to the pan. Season with salt and pepper, bring to the boil, then turn the heat down to a gentle simmer. Cover and simmer for 25–30 minutes, stirring often, until the lentils are cooked and the sauce is rich and syrupy. Check the seasoning and serve sprinkled with chopped parsley.

TO FREEZE,
Allow to cool completely, then transfer to an airtight container and freeze for up to 2 months. Defrost completely before reheating slowly until piping hot throughout.

Speedy beef stroganoff pies with a crunchy herb topping

Most beef stews need a long braise to achieve their full potential, but this stroganoff is made using thin strips of steak, so it's quick and easy. It's crowned with crunchy herbed breadcrumbs for extra deliciousness.

FEEDS 4 (EASILY DOUBLED)

FOR THE BREADCRUMB TOPPING
200g seeded bread
2 tbsp finely chopped flat-leaf parsley
1 tbsp olive oil
salt and black pepper to season

FOR THE FILLING
500g sirloin steak, trimmed and sliced
    into 5mm strips
2 tbsp olive oil
300g baby mushrooms, halved
2 small red onions, finely sliced
2 garlic cloves, crushed
1 red pepper, deseeded and thinly sliced
4 tsp plain flour
2 tsp paprika
500ml beef stock
2 tbsp tomato purée
3 tbsp soured cream

1   Preheat the oven to 200°C/180°C fan/ Gas mark 6 and grease 4 ovenproof dishes.

2   Place the bread, parsley and oil into a food processor and blitz into large crumbs. Season with salt and pepper and set aside.

3   Season the strips of steak well with salt and pepper.

4   Heat 1 tablespoon of the oil in a sauté pan or large, deep frying pan over a medium–high heat. Working in batches, add the beef, searing quickly until just coloured. Remove each batch with a slotted spatula and set aside while you sear the remainder.

5   Add the mushrooms to the hot pan and cook quickly until golden. Remove from the pan and set aside, leaving the pan on the heat.

6   Turn the heat down and pour the remaining oil into the pan. Add the onions, garlic and red pepper and fry gently for 8 minutes until the vegetables are soft.

7   Sprinkle the flour and paprika evenly over the top and stir for 2 minutes. Gradually add the beef stock and tomato purée, stirring continuously. Bring to the boil, then reduce the heat and simmer for 5 minutes until the sauce has thickened.

8   Tip the beef and mushrooms back into the pan and warm through gently. Taste and add more salt and pepper if needed, then stir in the soured cream.

9   Divide the stroganoff between the 4 dishes and scatter over the breadcrumbs. Bake for 15–20 minutes until the topping is crunchy and golden and the pies are cooked through.

TO FREEZE
Allow the pies to cool completely before covering tightly with foil. Freeze for up to 1 month. To cook, loosen the foil a little and bake in a preheated oven at 200°C/180°C fan/Gas mark 6 for 20 minutes. Remove the foil and bake for another 20–25 minutes until piping hot throughout.

One-pot quick fish curry with noodles and pak choi

Thanks to shop-bought curry paste, this spicy curry takes just minutes to throw together. It's cooked in one pot, so you won't have a kitchen full of dishes either. If you're making this in advance, leave out the noodles until you reheat to serve. You can replace the shallots and green curry paste with 2 tablespoons of homemade Thai base (see p.13) if you have some to hand.

FEEDS 4 (EASILY DOUBLED)

2 tbsp vegetable oil
2 large shallots, halved lengthways and
    finely sliced
4 tsp green curry paste
1 x 400ml tin of full-fat coconut milk
250ml chicken or vegetable stock
finely grated zest and juice of 1 lime
1 tbsp fish sauce
4 kaffir lime leaves
1–2 tsp light soy sauce
4 skinless, flaky white fish fillets
2 heads of pak choi, roughly chopped
1 green pepper, deseeded and finely sliced
300g fresh rice noodles
2 tbsp chopped coriander, to serve
1 red or green chilli, deseeded and
    finely chopped, to serve (optional)

1 Warm the oil in a large, deep frying pan or wok on a medium heat and add the shallots. Cook for 5 minutes, until softened but not browned, then add the green curry paste. Stir well and cook for another 3 minutes.

2 Add the coconut milk, stock, lime zest and juice, fish sauce, lime leaves and 1 teaspoon of soy sauce. Bring to the boil, reduce the heat and simmer for 5 minutes. Taste and add more soy sauce if needed.

3 Using a spatula, gently place the fish fillets, pak choi and slices of green pepper into the curry and poach the fish for 3–4 minutes until just cooked.

4 If you are eating immediately, add the rice noodles, being careful not to break up the fish, and heat through. Serve in warmed bowls sprinkled with chopped coriander, and with chilli, if you wish.

MAKE AHEAD
Once you've cooked the fish, allow it to cool completely. Cover and store in the fridge for up to 2 days. To reheat, add the fresh noodles and warm the sauce through without boiling until piping hot. Serve with the chopped coriander and the chilli if you wish.

Frozen honey-soy salmon parcels

Discovering you can cook fish from frozen is a life-changer in terms of saving time, and adding herbs and spices before the fillets hit the freezer makes frozen fish an even speedier supper. These salmon fillets are ready-prepped and just need a little decoration when they come out of the oven. Serve with your favourite stir-fried vegetables and simple jasmine rice.

FEEDS 8

2 tbsp sesame oil
8 salmon fillets
6 tbsp light soy sauce
4 tsp runny honey
large thumb-sized piece of fresh ginger,
    finely chopped
1 large red chilli, deseeded and finely sliced
3 tbsp finely chopped coriander
1 lemongrass stalk, very finely chopped

TO SERVE
sesame seeds
1 small bunch of spring onions, finely chopped
1 lime, quartered
jasmine rice (cooked) and stir-fried vegetables

1   Lay out 8 pieces of foil or greaseproof paper, each big enough to wrap a salmon fillet. Use some of the oil to lightly grease each piece. Place the fillets in the centre of each foil piece, and loosely gather up the edges to help contain the marinade.

2   Whisk the soy, honey and remaining oil together and pour equally over the fish. Sprinkle the remaining ingredients equally on top and bring the edges of the foil pieces together to seal each piece of salmon into a parcel.

TO FREEZE
Place each parcel the right way up in an airtight container and freeze for up to 2 months.

TO COOK
3   Preheat the oven to 180°C/160°C fan/ Gas mark 4.

4   Remove the salmon parcels from the freezer and place them on a baking tray. Roast in the preheated oven for 25–30 minutes until cooked through.

5   To serve, open the parcels carefully (the steam will be very hot), sprinkle with sesame seeds and spring onions, and squeeze over a little lime. Serve with jasmine rice and stir-fried vegetables.

Cooking for a crowd might require a bigger shopping trolley but that doesn't mean you have to compromise on flavour. Get ahead by cooking your favourite big batches in advance and you can enjoy the party too.

5 | Family friendly – big batches to feed eight or more

Whether you regularly feed hordes of hungry people or have suddenly been roped in to host a big family event, cooking in bulk can be hard work, both in terms of logistics and time. The trick to enjoying the process and producing fabulous food that everyone will love is simply to plan ahead and give yourself plenty of time when you have it.

In many ways, big batches are where this book began. Alongside make-ahead meals for busy days, most batch cooking is about making food to feed a crowd, either in a single sitting for a big group around the table, or for a small family to eat over several days (with a little help from the fridge or freezer). Cooking for bigger groups is more time-consuming, and if they're your favourite people too, it makes perfect sense to get ahead of yourself and cook in advance, so you can enjoy their company instead of toiling in the kitchen while everyone else parties.

So this chapter is all about hearty dishes you can make in advance – big and breezy, lip-smackingly delicious recipes that will all feed at least eight people.

And if your crowd is even bigger, check out the mega-lasagne recipes. Lasagne is a classic make-ahead party food, but it's often hard to find a good recipe that is generous enough to feed a room full of hungry people. These meat and plant-based beauties take a little effort to prepare but can be made well ahead of the main event. In return for your hard work they'll keep 10–12 munchers happy and portions freeze well if you need an ongoing supply of your favourite pasta bake.

If you're a fan of the traybake, try the Baked cardamom chicken curry (see p.114) or Honey, soy and five-spice baked chicken (p.117), both of which are made in a single baking tin with the teeniest amount of preparation, yet are guaranteed to have your guests asking you for the recipe. And if you like to linger, the West African pork and peanut stew (see p.122) is a slow-cooker classic that reheats beautifully (if there is any left, of course).

These dishes use many different cooking techniques to produce a diverse range of flavours and textures. And as you can do most of the work ahead of the main event, they're guaranteed to keep both you and your favourite people in the party spirit.

The best family friendly big batches

Baked cardamom chicken curry

Honey, soy and five-spice baked chicken

Chicken and ham hock pot pies

Slow-cooked mustard and maple pulled pork with fennel slaw

Slow-cooked West African pork and peanut stew with black-eyed beans

Luxury budget fish cakes with mustard and chive sauce

Roasted Gujarati salmon fillet with sweet potato and peas

Lamb, wild garlic and mint burgers

Big beef, thyme and sneaky lentil lasagne

Giant roasted vegetable lasagne

Classic big batch beef and butternut stew

Baked cardamom chicken curry

Baked curry is my go-to dish when I'm tight on time with a big crowd to feed. It needs very little preparation and the marinade turns into a delicious sauce all by itself, which means no stirring. It's also a good one to make in advance, as it will gladly wait in the fridge for a while until you're ready to cook. This is a generous curry, which can be halved, but I'd suggest making the lot and keeping leftovers in the fridge for another day. Serve with rice and the usual curry accompaniments.

FEEDS 8

2kg skin-on, bone-in chicken thighs
2 tsp Maldon salt, plus extra to season
generous grinding of black pepper,
    plus extra to season
finely grated zest and juice of 2 lemons
large thumb-sized piece of fresh ginger, grated
6 garlic cloves, crushed
2 tbsp ground coriander
4 tsp ground cumin
1 tsp chilli flakes
1 tsp turmeric
10 cardamom pods, seeds crushed,
    husks discarded
2 cinnamon sticks
6 cloves
200g natural yoghurt
2 tbsp vegetable oil, for roasting
2 onions, finely chopped
4 large handfuls of spinach, washed
rice, naan bread and chutneys, to serve

1   In a large ovenproof casserole dish or deep roasting tin, place the chicken, salt, black pepper and lemon zest and juice. Mix well, cover and set aside for 30 minutes.

2   Mix the ginger, garlic and remaining dried spices with the yoghurt and add this to the chicken. Stir well so that the chicken pieces are evenly coated, cover and refrigerate for a minimum of 30 minutes or up to 24 hours.

3   Preheat the oven to 180°C/160°C fan/ Gas mark 4.

4   When you are ready to cook, uncover the chicken and brush with the oil. Sprinkle the chopped onions evenly over the top.

5   Roast the chicken for 50 minutes, then baste with the juices and chopped onions and increase the heat to 200°C/180°C fan/Gas mark 6. Roast for another 30–40 minutes, basting halfway through, until the chicken is cooked through and the skin is crispy. Move the chicken pieces around in the dish or tin if the pieces at the edges are cooking faster than the ones in the middle.

6   Remove from the oven and stir in the spinach until it wilts. Serve with rice, naan breads and chutneys.

TO FEED 4
If you are cooking half the quantity of chicken, cook for 40 minutes, then increase the heat to 200°C/180°C fan/Gas mark 6 and cook for 20–30 minutes, basting occasionally, until the meat is cooked through and the skin is crispy.

Honey, soy and five-spice baked chicken

This is a quick and stress-free supper that will happily feed a crowd or make two delicious meals for four people. Chicken thigh meat is very moist and will be full of flavour from the marinade, so any leftovers make a great base for quick stir-fries. You can marinate the chicken for as little as 30 minutes or leave it overnight if you are getting organised. Serve with rice or noodles.

FEEDS 8 (EASILY HALVED OR DOUBLED)

1 tsp 5-spice powder
4 tbsp light soy sauce
3 tbsp runny honey
1 tbsp vegetable oil
1 red chilli, deseeded and finely chopped
5 garlic cloves, crushed
40g fresh ginger, peeled and grated
2kg skin-on, bone-in chicken thighs
bunch of spring onions, trimmed and
    finely chopped
2 big handfuls of coriander leaves
2 tsp sesame seeds

1 Whisk the 5-spice, soy sauce, honey and oil together in a large bowl. Stir in the chilli, garlic and ginger. Add the chicken thighs and turn them over in the marinade, using your hands, until they are evenly coated. Leave to marinate for at least 30 minutes.

2 Preheat the oven to 200°C/180°C fan/Gas mark 6 and grease a roasting tin large enough for the chicken to fit snugly inside.

3 Place the thighs, skin sides upwards, in the roasting tin and pour over the marinade. Roast for 40 minutes, basting halfway through, then increase the heat to 220°C/200°C fan/Gas mark 7 for another 20–25 minutes until the skin is deliciously crispy.

4 To serve, scatter with spring onions, coriander leaves and sesame seeds and drizzle with any remaining sauce from the tin.

LEFTOVERS
Strip any leftover chicken from the bone and store it in an airtight container with any extra sauce. Allow to cool completely, then refrigerate for up to 2 days and use as a base for a delicious chicken stir-fry.

Chicken and ham hock pot pies

Pies are the ultimate comfort food. Having one all to yourself is the culinary equivalent of a cosy sofa in front of a roaring fire. You can freeze these cute pot pies for days when you need a little succour. The recipe makes 8 portions (if you can bear to share, that is).

50g butter, plus extra for greasing
4 leeks, thinly sliced
3 celery sticks, finely diced
3 tsp thyme leaves
2kg skinless, boneless chicken thighs, cut into bite-sized chunks
4 tbsp plain flour
200ml white wine
500ml chicken stock
150ml double cream
250g cooked ham hock, shredded
finely grated zest of 2 lemons
3 tbsp finely chopped chives
2 sheets of ready-rolled puff pastry
1 egg, beaten
salt and black pepper to season

1 Grease 8 small ovenproof dishes or deep foil trays.

2 Melt the butter in a large heavy-based casserole or saucepan, and add the leeks, celery, thyme and a good seasoning of salt. Cook for 10 minutes until the leeks are softened but not browned, then add the chicken and stir regularly for 15–20 minutes until lightly cooked.

3 Turn up the heat and sprinkle over the flour. Mix well, pour in the wine and stir until it's absorbed. Stir in the stock until the sauce is smooth and shiny and simmer gently for 10 minutes. Stir in the cream and warm through without boiling.

4 Remove from the heat and stir in the ham, lemon zest and chopped chives. Taste and add more salt and pepper if required, then pour the pie filling into your chosen dishes. (See freezer notes now if you intend to freeze.)

5 Unroll the puff pastry sheets and cut eight 'lids' to fit the pie dishes or foil trays. Tidy the edges and use any trimmings to decorate the tops of the pies.

6 To bake the pies, preheat the oven to 200°C/180°C fan/Gas mark 6.

7 Egg wash the top of each pie and cut a slit to allow steam to escape. Bake for 30–35 minutes. Cover loosely with foil if the top starts to look too brown.

TO FREEZE
Allow the filling to cool completely in the pie dishes before covering with the pastry lids. Wrap the lidded pies in foil and freeze for up to 1 month. To bake from frozen, preheat the oven to 180°C/160°C fan/Gas mark 4, egg wash the tops and bake for 40–45 minutes until golden brown and piping hot throughout.

Slow-cooked mustard and maple pulled pork with fennel slaw

Slow cooking is a revelation when it comes to pulled pork. With just a few minutes' prep, you can create a meal that tastes as if you've been slaving away for hours in the kitchen. It's planet-friendly too as the slow cooker uses much less energy than an oven.

FEEDS 8

5 tbsp wholegrain mustard
1 tbsp English mustard powder
4 tbsp maple syrup
½ tsp smoked paprika
1.8kg pork shoulder, in one piece
salt and black pepper to season
16 tortilla wraps, warmed, to serve
2 tbsp chopped flat-leaf parsley, to serve

FOR THE FENNEL SLAW
2 tbsp red wine vinegar
1 tbsp olive oil
1 tbsp runny honey
1 tbsp flat-leaf parsley, finely chopped
1 large fennel bulb, trimmed, cored, halved
    and sliced paper thin
½ red cabbage, cored and finely shredded

1 Mix the mustards, maple syrup and paprika together and tip into a slow cooker.

2 If the pork shoulder has been rolled and tied, remove the string. Cut off the rind. Place the pork in the slow cooker and massage the marinade into the meat with your hands. Season generously with salt and pepper. Cook on low for 6–7 hours until tender.

3 At least an hour before the pork is finished, make the fennel slaw. Whisk the vinegar, oil, honey and parsley together and season generously with salt and pepper. Add the fennel and cabbage, stir well and leave for at least 1 hour, while the pork finishes cooking.

4 When the pork is ready, remove it from the slow cooker and shred the meat. Pour over enough of the juices from the slow cooker to keep it moist but don't let it swim in the liquid.

5 Serve the pork warm in tortilla wraps, scattered with parsley and a big helping of fennel slaw.

LEFTOVERS
Keep any uneaten pulled pork in the fridge for up to 3 days. It makes a great filling for toasted sandwiches, or a base for pasta sauces and stir-fries.

Slow-cooked West African pork and peanut stew with black-eyed beans

Sometimes a recipe is so good you know you will make it again and again. This is one of those. It was on the menu in a local pub, and the chef said his secret was a homemade pork broth cooked over four days. My slow-cooker version cheats with a chicken stock cube, but still has an incredible depth of flavour and a subtle heat. All you'll need alongside are some simple grains or just plain old rice. It might seem like a lot of ingredients, but once it's in the slow cooker, your work is done.

FEEDS 8

1.8kg trimmed pork shoulder,
    cut into 3–4cm pieces
2–3 tbsp vegetable oil
1 large onion, finely chopped
2 green peppers, deseeded and roughly chopped
4 garlic cloves, crushed
1 tsp ground cumin
2 tsp ground coriander
1 tsp curry powder
1 tsp cayenne pepper
¼ tsp or a generous pinch of ground cloves
4 tbsp tomato purée
2 x 400g tins of chopped tomatoes
300ml chicken stock
100g salted peanuts
6 tbsp peanut butter
2 x 400g tins of black-eyed beans
salt and black pepper to season
finely grated zest and juice of 1 lemon, to serve
2 tbsp chopped flat-leaf parsley (optional),
    to serve
rice, quinoa or couscous, cooked, to serve

1   Season the pork with salt and pepper.

2   Heat 2 tablespoons of oil in a large non-stick frying pan on a medium–high heat and quickly brown the pork in batches until golden on all sides. Transfer the meat to a slow cooker using a slotted spoon.

3   Add the onion, peppers and garlic to the pan and cook for 8 minutes, until soft but not browned, adding a little more vegetable oil if needed.

4   Add the spices and tomato purée and cook for another 2 minutes. Pour in the chopped tomatoes and chicken stock and bring to the boil.

5   Carefully pour the stew into the slow cooker and stir in the peanuts. Cover and cook on low for 5–6 hours until tender.

6   30 minutes before you want to eat, remove a mug of sauce from the stew. Pour a little into the peanut butter and mix well. Gradually add the remaining sauce in the mug until you have a smooth sauce.

7 Stir the peanut butter sauce back into the stew, add the black-eyed beans and cook on high for 15–30 minutes until the beans are cooked through and the stew is rich and thick. (See notes now if you intend to freeze.)

8 Before serving, taste and add more salt and pepper if needed, stir through the lemon zest and juice, and sprinkle with parsley. Serve with rice, quinoa or couscous.

MAKE AHEAD
Allow the stew to cool completely, transfer to an airtight container and refrigerate for up to 2 days or freeze for up to 2 months. Defrost, if necessary, before reheating gently and slowly until piping hot throughout.

Luxury budget fishcakes with mustard and chive sauce

These fishcakes taste ridiculously luxurious but they're actually made with a regular supermarket fish-pie mixture. They are rich and filling, with a sharp mustard and chive sauce. Simple green vegetables such as broccoli, peas or spinach would be the ideal accompaniment.

FEEDS 8

FOR THE FISHCAKES
550g large white potatoes, whole and unpeeled
800g fresh fish pie mixture
    (chopped fish only, no shellfish or squid)
500ml milk
1 tbsp wholegrain mustard
2 bay leaves
4 eggs
8 spring onions, very finely chopped
large bunch of flat-leaf parsley, leaves
    picked and chopped
120g mature cheddar, grated
finely grated zest of 1 lemon
plain flour, for dusting
150g fine dried breadcrumbs or panko
    breadcrumbs
sunflower oil, for frying
salt and black pepper to season

FOR THE MUSTARD AND CHIVE SAUCE
40g butter
40g plain flour
1 tbsp wholegrain mustard
3 tbsp finely chopped chives
juice of 1 lemon

1   Microwave bake the potatoes until soft. Spoon the flesh out of the skins into a large bowl. Lightly mash and allow to cool.

2   While the potatoes are baking and cooling, put the fish, milk, mustard and bay leaves into a saucepan and slowly heat until simmering. Turn the heat off, cover and leave to cool for 10 minutes. Strain and reserve the liquid for the sauce. (If you intend to make the fishcakes for freezing, you can freeze the liquid, then defrost to make the sauce as needed.)

3   Beat 1 egg and add it to the cooled potatoes with the spring onions, parsley and cheese. Stir in the lemon zest and season with salt and pepper.

4   Gently flake the strained fish into the potato mixture and combine carefully, keeping the flakes intact as much as possible. Using damp hands, shape the mixture into 8 thick, round fishcakes.

5   Beat the remaining eggs in a bowl. Tip the flour into a separate bowl and the breadcrumbs into another.

6 Place a fishcake into the flour bowl, dusting it all over, then move it to the beaten egg, turning it over to coat on all sides. Finally, dip it into the breadcrumbs and turn, ensuring it is covered with a fine layer of crumbs. Set aside and repeat with the rest of the fishcakes. (See freezer notes now if you intend to freeze the fishcakes.) If eating immediately, put the fishcakes to one side while you make the sauce.

7 To make the mustard and chive sauce, melt the butter gently with the flour in a saucepan and stir until you have a golden paste. Add the strained poaching liquid a little at a time, stirring continuously. When the sauce has thickened, add the mustard, chives, and 1 tablespoon of the lemon juice (add the remaining juice to a glass of water for a refreshing drink). Season to taste, then cover and keep warm while you cook the fishcakes.

8 Cook the fishcakes in batches. Heat 3 tablespoons of oil in a large frying pan and cook each batch for 4–6 minutes on each side until golden. Add more oil if needed. Serve with peas, spinach, or pea shoots and a bowl of sauce for spooning over.

TO FREEZE

If you are not eating all the fishcakes immediately, freeze them after coating. Place them between layers of greaseproof paper in an airtight container or freezer bags and freeze for up to 1 month. Cook from frozen as described in the method, but with a longer cooking time of 8–10 minutes each side, until piping hot throughout.

You can also freeze any leftover sauce. Allow to cool completely, then transfer to an airtight container or freezer bag and freeze for up to 1 month. Defrost and reheat very slowly until piping hot throughout.

Roasted Gujarati salmon fillet with sweet potato and peas

This is a bold and happy meal, full of sunny rainbow vegetables and moist, flaky fish. The whole dish is cooked in a large roasting tin, and requires just a few minutes of prep and occasional stirring. Add leftovers to salads or gently stir them through couscous or other grains. You'll need a very large roasting tin or 2 smaller tins.

FEEDS 8

4 tbsp coconut or olive oil, plus extra
    for drizzling
600g potatoes, peeled and cut into
    1cm cubes
800g sweet potatoes, peeled and cut into
    1cm cubes
2 red onions, each cut into 8 segments
1 large red pepper, deseeded and cut
    into chunks
1 large yellow pepper, deseeded and cut
    into chunks
2 x 500g skin-on salmon fillets (de-boned
    half sides)
1 tbsp Gujarati spice paste or 2 tbsp tandoori
    spice paste
300g baby spinach
200g frozen peas
salt and black pepper to season
2 large handfuls of coriander, leaves picked,
    to serve
2 lemons, quartered, to serve

1 Preheat the oven to 200°C/180°C fan/ Gas mark 6.

2 Add the oil to the roasting tin and add the potatoes, sweet potatoes, and onions. Season generously with salt and pepper and turn the potatoes so they are coated with oil. Roast for 40 minutes, turning halfway through, then add the peppers and roast for another 15 minutes until the potatoes are golden around the edges.

3 Lightly score a cross-cross pattern on the top of the salmon fillets, then brush them with spice paste and drizzle with oil.

4 Remove the roasting tin from the oven and mix the spinach and frozen peas through the potatoes, until the spinach wilts.

5 Place the salmon fillets, skin sides downwards, on top of the vegetables and return to the oven for 20–25 minutes, until the salmon is just cooked. Remove from the oven, season with salt and pepper and scatter with coriander. Place the lemon wedges around the edges and serve straight from the tin.

LEFTOVERS
Allow to cool completely, transfer to an airtight container and refrigerate for up to 2 days, then enjoy cold with a salad or grains.

Lamb, wild garlic and mint burgers

These are a great alternative to traditional beef burgers. Wild garlic has a short season, but it has a lovely gentle flavour that goes beautifully with lamb. If you can't find it, make these anyway as the burgers will have a delicious minty twist. Fire up the BBQ, cook your patties and serve them up with melted cheese, sliced gherkins, roasted peppers and a dollop of your favourite relish for an instant feast.

MAKES 8

1kg minced lamb
150g fine fresh, dried or frozen breadcrumbs
2 tbsp finely chopped wild garlic
2 tbsp chopped mint leaves
5 spring onions, finely chopped
finely grated zest of 1 lemon
8 thick slices of cheddar
salt and black pepper to season

TO SERVE
8 large burger buns, halved
4 large gherkins, finely sliced lengthways
4 roasted peppers, drained and cut in half
burger relish of choice

1   Mix the lamb, breadcrumbs, wild garlic, mint, spring onions and lemon zest together. Season generously with salt and pepper. Shape into 8 wide, flat, equal-sized patties. Refrigerate for 30 minutes before cooking. (See freezer notes now if you intend to freeze.)

2   Heat a barbecue or grill to hot. Cook the burgers on the barbecue for 3–4 minutes on each side, or under the grill for 7–8 minutes each side. Top each burger with a slice of cheese and cook for a few seconds until melted.

3   To serve, place each patty in a burger bun with sliced gherkins, roasted peppers and a big dollop of relish.

TO FREEZE
Place the uncooked burgers between layers of greaseproof paper or reusable liners and wrap in foil. Freeze in an airtight container for up to 2 months. Defrost before cooking and serving as described in the method.

Big beef, thyme and sneaky lentil lasagne

The quintessential lasagne is most definitely a big one. Not only is this bubbling, golden pasta bake a thing of beauty, super-sizing it makes the lengthy preparation worthwhile. Use this mammoth lasagne to feed a crowd or portion it for the fridge or freezer to delight and satisfy for days to come. Although it's heavy on the vegetables and sneaks in a few pulses, it is ultimately a rich, meaty dish, which will keep everyone very happy. If you already have some white sauce (see p.18) in the freezer, use this as the basis for your cheese sauce – simply defrost, reheat and add the cheese.

FEEDS 8–10

3 tbsp olive oil
2 onions, finely chopped
4 garlic cloves, crushed
2 carrots, peeled, quartered and
    finely chopped
2 leeks, finely sliced
200g medium-sized mushrooms,
    halved and sliced
1kg minced beef
200g red lentils
3 x 400g tins of chopped tomatoes
400ml beef stock
3 tbsp tomato purée
4 tsp thyme leaves
2 dried bay leaves
2 tsp dried oregano
12–15 fresh lasagne sheets
50g mature cheddar, grated
salt and black pepper to season

FOR THE CHEESE SAUCE
80g butter
80g plain flour
1 litre milk
250g mature cheddar, grated

1   Heat 2 tablespoons of oil in a large casserole or sauté pan on a medium heat and add the onions, garlic, carrots and leeks. Fry for 10–12 minutes until the onions are very soft but not browned, then remove with a slotted spatula and set aside. Quickly fry the mushrooms over a hot heat until lightly browned. Remove and set aside.

2   Add the remaining oil to the pan and cook the minced beef in batches until browned all over. Return the cooked vegetables and all the beef to the pan and stir in the lentils.

3   Pour in the chopped tomatoes and beef stock and add the tomato purée. Tip the thyme, bay leaves and oregano into the pan, stir, then season well with salt and pepper.

4   Bring to the boil, then turn the heat down and simmer for 60 minutes, stirring occasionally and adding a little water if the mixture looks too dry.

5 While it's simmering, make the cheese sauce. Melt the butter gently in a saucepan with the flour until they form a golden paste. Gradually whisk in the milk, a little at a time, until there are no lumps. Bring gently to the boil, stirring until the sauce has thickened. Turn off the heat and mix in the grated cheese to melt. Cover with a lid and set aside.

6 To cook, preheat the oven to 180°C/160°C fan/ Gas mark 4 and grease a large, shallow casserole or baking dish approximately 34cm x 28cm.

7 Spoon a quarter of the meat sauce across the bottom of the baking dish and cover it with a single layer of pasta, trimming to fit the shape of your dish, if necessary.

8 Pour a third of the cheese sauce over the lasagne sheets and smooth it evenly across the pasta.

9 Repeat the layers of meat, pasta and cheese sauce, finishing with sauce on the top. Scatter the grated cheese over the top. (See freezer notes now if you intend to make ahead or freeze.)

10 Cook for 60–70 minutes until golden on top. If the top looks as if it is starting to burn, cover it loosely with foil.

TO MAKE AHEAD OR FREEZE

You can make this lasagne in advance and store it before cooking. Cool the constructed lasagne completely and cover with foil before storing in the fridge for up to 2 days, or in the freezer for up to 1 month.

Remove the foil and cook for another 20–40 minutes until piping hot and nicely golden on top. Alternatively, cut the uncooked lasagne into single portions and freeze the portions in smaller dishes. Cook from frozen using a shorter cooking time.

Giant roasted vegetable lasagne

Vegetable lasagne is all-too-often full of overcooked, indistinguishable veg in gloomy, watery sauces. The key to avoiding this and creating a firm, flavoursome dish is to cook the key ingredients separately. It does take more time, but this is a lavish bake that feeds a crowd, so it's worth it. Make sure you prepare the ingredients in advance so you can multi-task on sauces while the vegetables are roasting. If you already have some white sauce (see p.18) in the freezer, use this as the basis for your cheese sauce – simply defrost, reheat and add the cheese.

FEEDS 10

2 aubergines, sliced lengthways into 6–8 slices
2 large courgettes (about 750g), sliced
    lengthways into 6–8 thick slices
4 tbsp olive oil
30g butter
800g medium-sized mushrooms, thickly sliced
2 onions, finely chopped
4 garlic cloves, finely chopped
½ tsp chilli flakes
1 tsp dried oregano
2 tbsp tomato purée
3 x 400g tins of chopped tomatoes
1 tsp sugar or runny honey
12–15 fresh lasagne sheets
salt and black pepper to season

FOR THE CHEESE SAUCE
80g butter
80g plain flour
1 litre milk
300g mature cheddar, grated

1   Preheat the oven to 180°C/160°C fan/ Gas mark 4.

2   Place the sliced aubergines and courgettes on large baking trays lined with greaseproof paper or reusable liners. Drizzle over 3 tablespoons of olive oil and season generously with salt and pepper. Roast for 40 minutes until soft and lightly golden.

3   While the vegetables are roasting, melt the butter in a large, deep sauté pan or shallow casserole and add a generous seasoning of salt and pepper. On a high heat, fry the mushrooms in batches until brown and crispy around the edges. Remove the mushrooms with a slotted spoon and set aside.

4   In the same pan, fry the onions, garlic and chilli flakes in the remaining oil for 8 minutes, until the onions are softened. Add the oregano, tomato purée, chopped tomatoes, half a tin of water and the sugar or honey, and bring to the boil. Turn the heat down and leave to simmer gently for 30 minutes until thick and syrupy. Season with salt and pepper to taste, then stir in the mushrooms and set aside to cool.

5 To make the cheese sauce, melt the butter gently in a saucepan with the flour until they form a golden paste. Gradually add the milk, whisking continuously, then bring to the boil and keep stirring until the sauce is smooth and thick.

6 Set aside 2 handfuls of grated cheese for the top of the lasagne and stir the rest into the sauce. Turn off the heat, cover with a lid and set aside.

7 Grease a large, deep ovenproof dish or baking tin (approximately 34cm x 28cm). Ladle one third of the tomato and mushroom sauce into the dish and place a single layer of aubergine and courgette slices over the top.

8 Cover with a layer of fresh lasagne sheets (trimming to fit the shape of your dish, if necessary), then add a third of the cheese sauce. Repeat the layers, finishing with the last of the cheese sauce. Scatter the reserved grated cheese over the top. (See notes now if you're making in advance or intend to freeze.)

9 Bake for 50–60 minutes until piping hot, bubbling and golden brown. (Alternatively, construct the lasagne along the same layering principles in several smaller ovenproof dishes and cook for 40–45 minutes, until bubbling and golden brown.)

TO MAKE AHEAD OR FREEZE

To make in advance, allow the constructed lasagne to cool completely, then cover with foil. Refrigerate for 2 days or freeze for up to 1 month. Bake (defrosting first, if necessary) as instructed in the recipe method. You can also freeze the lasagne in separate portions, with a shorter cooking time.

Classic big batch beef and butternut stew

When it comes to batch cooking, a substantial stew is top of my list. It's one of those dishes that takes little preparation and will happily cook away all by itself for hours. When it's done, you can eat your heart out (the smell will be so tempting you won't be able to resist) and you can batch up the rest for the fridge or freezer. Eat with mashed potato, rice or simple hunks of crusty bread.

FEEDS 8–10

3 tbsp plain flour
¼ tsp cayenne pepper
1.6kg braising steak, trimmed and chopped
    into bite-sized pieces
4–5 tbsp olive oil
3 onions, finely chopped
150g baby mushrooms, halved
2 celery sticks, finely chopped
4 garlic cloves, crushed
4 carrots, peeled and thickly sliced
3 tsp dried oregano
3 bay leaves
150ml red wine
5 tbsp tomato purée
2 x 400g tins of chopped tomatoes
1 litre beef stock
700g butternut squash, peeled, deseeded and
    chopped into 3cm chunks
finely grated zest and juice of 1 lemon
salt and black pepper to season
mashed potato, rice or crusty bread, to serve

1   Mix the flour and cayenne pepper in a large bowl and season with salt and pepper. Add the meat and toss until it is lightly coated in the seasoned flour.

2   Pour 2 tablespoons of oil into a large ovenproof casserole over a medium–high heat. Add the beef and fry in batches until browned all over, adding a little more oil as needed. Transfer each batch to a plate with a slotted spoon as soon as it is cooked.

3   Turn the heat down and add the remaining oil to the casserole. Tip in the onions, mushrooms, celery, garlic, carrots, oregano and bay leaves. Cook for 10–12 minutes until the onions are soft but not browned.

4   Preheat the oven to 160°C/140°C fan/ Gas mark 2–3.

5   Turn the heat up, then return the beef to the casserole and pour over the wine. Stir, then add the tomato purée, chopped tomatoes and beef stock. Bring to the boil, cover with a tight-fitting lid, then transfer to the oven and cook for 2 hours.

6   Add the chopped butternut and cook for another 1 hour, removing the lid for the last 20 minutes to allow the sauce to reduce. Taste and add more salt and pepper if needed. Before serving, stir in the lemon zest and 1 tablespoon of the juice (add the remaining juice to a glass of water for a refreshing drink).

TO FREEZE
Allow the stew to cool completely. Transfer to airtight containers and freeze for up to 2 months. Defrost and then warm slowly in a saucepan until piping hot.

Here comes the sun. With a little preparation and a stack of creative batch-cook recipes you can enjoy the taste of seasonal veggies all year round.

6 | Vegan and vegetarian batches — vibrant plant-based main meals and sides

There's nothing quite as delicious as fresh vegetables picked and eaten in season. Luckily for us, capturing and holding on to those incredible flavours is not as hard as you might think.

When I was researching this book, the most requested recipes from my volunteer testers were for vegan and vegetarian batches, especially from those testers who were trying to introduce more plant-based dishes into their diets. They struggled to come up with quick and varied meals day after day, especially when pushed for time, and were hugely disappointed by the vegetarian ready meals available. So the challenge was on to create deeply flavoursome dishes that would hold their flavour in the fridge or freezer.

It's a myth that only some vegetables freeze well. Rather, the truth is that, apart from a few (I'm talking about you, lettuce), many veggies and plant-based dishes hold their flavour and texture brilliantly. And as vegetables tend to arrive in big seasonal gluts in our gardens, markets and shops, batch cooking is a particularly efficient and budget-friendly way to take advantage of any deluge.

It's also a good method for dealing with preparation phobia. While many of us find peeling and chopping strangely therapeutic, not everyone feels the same, and vegetables can be particularly demanding. The good news is that, although it's true that batch cooking is initially more labour intensive, you're doing the work for several meals in advance, so your preparation time is concentrated into chunks, leaving your evenings free to enjoy the results.

So, whether you're already vegetarian or vegan, or just want to include more plant-based dishes into your diet, these riotously colourful make-ahead recipes will keep you happy, healthily fed and full. And thanks to their gorgeous rainbow shades, this chapter is full of light and colour. From bright orange, soft sweet potato falafels and emerald green 'raw' spinach and feta pies, to comforting and richly red, spiced coconut lentils, or thick celeriac steaks, roasted and served in a citrusy green and yellow soup, dive in and warm yourself in the glow of nature's most vibrant hues.

The best vegan and vegetarian batches

Thai-spiced pumpkin soup

Smoky aubergine and fennel tagine

Sweet potato and coriander falafels

Roasted celeriac laksa with lemongrass and lime

Speedy spinach and feta triangles

Chipotle, sun-dried tomato and sunshine pepper paella

Squash, pine nut and harissa 'sausage' rolls

Parsnip and cumin rostis

Stuffed gem squash with goat's cheese, walnuts and honey

Spiced red lentils with coconut and lime

Herby butter bean and kale stew

Sunny butternut and sweet potato gratin

Fast and furious quinoa 'bolognese'

Thai-spiced pumpkin soup

This is a feisty, colourful soup that is full of flavour. Using shop-bought red curry paste means it's quick to put together, and the coconut milk brings a luxurious richness that is perfect for chilly days when you want to be warmed from the inside. It's also particularly useful for recycling discarded Halloween pumpkins.

FEEDS 4–6

1kg pumpkin or butternut squash, skin on, deseeded and cut into large pieces
2 tbsp vegetable oil
2 garlic cloves, roughly chopped
1 onion, finely sliced
1 large thumb-sized piece of fresh ginger, peeled and grated
2 tbsp Thai red curry paste
500ml vegetable or chicken stock
1 x 400ml tin of full- or reduced-fat coconut milk
1 tsp caster sugar
light soy sauce, to taste
salt and black pepper to season
large handful of coriander, leaves picked and chopped, to serve
finely grated zest and juice of 1 lime, to serve
optional garnish: chopped red chilli, chilli oil, kaffir lime leaves and finely chopped spring onion

1   Preheat the oven to 180°C/160°C fan/ Gas mark 4.

2   Toss the pumpkin in a roasting tray with 1 tablespoon of the oil and the chopped garlic. Season with salt and pepper and roast for 45 minutes until softened. Remove from the oven and scrape the pumpkin flesh into a bowl, discarding the skin. Roughly mash the pumpkin and set aside.

3   Heat the remaining oil in a heavy-based saucepan over a medium heat and gently fry the onion for 7–8 minutes until soft. Turn up the heat a little, add the ginger and curry paste, and fry for 2–3 minutes. Add the stock, coconut milk and mashed pumpkin. Bring to the boil, then reduce the heat and simmer very gently for 10 minutes until the flavours have combined. Stir in the sugar, and add soy sauce to taste.

4   To serve, ladle into a bowl, and sprinkle with coriander leaves, and the lime zest and juice. Add the chilli and a drizzle of chilli oil if you like things spicy and garnish with kaffir lime leaves and chopped spring onions.

TO FREEZE
Allow the soup to cool completely, then transfer to an airtight container and freeze for up to 1 month. Defrost and reheat very gently to prevent the soup from splitting, until piping hot throughout.

Smoky aubergine and fennel tagine

I created this dish as the vegan alternative to beef stew for a bonfire-night crowd. The brief was for something hearty, warming, rich and fragrant that could be made in advance and reheated just before everyone rushed through the door. It makes a generous amount, but freezes well. It is simple, nourishing and utterly delicious. Eat on its own for a light meal or with plain couscous or rice.

FEEDS 6

2 tsp fennel seeds
2 tsp ground cumin
2 tsp ground coriander
1 tsp smoked paprika
1 tsp turmeric
2 cinnamon sticks
4 tbsp olive oil
2 aubergines, trimmed and cut into 1cm cubes
1 red onion, finely chopped
300g fennel, halved, trimmed and thinly sliced, fronds reserved
3 garlic cloves, crushed
1 red chilli, deseeded and finely chopped
2 x 400g tins of chopped tomatoes
250ml vegetable stock
1 tsp runny honey
2 x 400g tins of chickpeas, drained and rinsed
finely grated zest and juice of 1 lemon
salt and black pepper to season
rice or couscous, cooked, to serve

1   Dry-fry the fennel seeds over a medium–high heat until they start jumping in the pan, then crush them in a pestle and mortar. Place the crushed fennel in a small bowl with the cumin, coriander, paprika, turmeric and cinnamon sticks.

2   In a large, deep, frying pan or cast-iron casserole, heat 3 tablespoons of the olive oil over a medium–high heat until very hot. Fry the aubergine quickly until lightly golden brown all over. Remove the cubes and set aside.

3   Turn the heat down and add the remaining oil, along with the onion, fennel, garlic and chilli. Cook gently for 6–8 minutes until soft, then add the bowl of spices and cook for 2 minutes.

4   Tip the aubergine cubes back into the pan along with the tomatoes and stock. Bring to the boil, turn down the heat and simmer gently for 20–25 minutes until the sauce is reduced. Stir in the honey and season to taste with salt and pepper.

5   Add the chickpeas and cook for 8–10 minutes until warmed through, then add the lemon zest and juice. Sprinkle with the reserved fennel fronds and serve with rice or couscous.

TO FREEZE
Cool the tagine completely and transfer it to airtight bags or boxes. Freeze for up to 2 months. Defrost, then reheat slowly until piping hot throughout.

Sweet potato and coriander falafels

These light sweet potato falafels are much lower in fat than traditional deep-fried versions. Making them by hand, rather than in a food processor, gives them a chunkier texture than traditional falafels. They make great snacks on their own or a light meal with warm pitta bread, salad, pickles and chilli sauce. The uncooked falafels freeze very well.

MAKES 25–30

700g sweet potatoes
200g potatoes
1 x 400g tin of chickpeas, drained and rinsed
3 tbsp plain or gram flour
1 garlic clove, crushed
1 tsp ground coriander
2 tsp ground cumin
4 tbsp finely chopped coriander leaves
3 tbsp lemon juice
1 tbsp tahini
½ tsp salt, plus extra to season if needed
generous grinding of black pepper, plus extra
    to season if needed
olive oil, for brushing
1 tbsp sesame seeds
warmed pitta breads, to serve
salad, pickles and chilli sauce, to serve

1 Microwave both types of potato in their jackets on full power until cooked through (this will take 5–10 minutes per potato, depending on size), or bake them in the oven at 200°C/180°C fan/Gas mark 6 for 1 hour –1 hour 30 minutes, and leave to cool completely.

2 Mash the drained chickpeas in a bowl with a fork or potato masher. Add the potato flesh and gently stir it into the mashed chickpeas.

3 Add all the other ingredients except the oil for brushing and the sesame seeds and mix well. Taste and add a little more seasoning if needed.

4 Using your hands, roll the mixture into 25–30 equal, walnut-sized balls and place them on a baking tray lined with greaseproof paper or a reusable baking sheet. (See freezer notes now if you intend to freeze.)

5 If you're baking the falafels straight away, preheat the oven to 200°C/180°C fan/Gas mark 6. Brush them with a little oil, sprinkle with sesame seeds and bake for 25–30 minutes, turning halfway through the cooking time, until nicely crispy all over the outside.

TO FREEZE
If you're freezing the falafels, open freeze them first by placing the tray in the freezer for 30–40 minutes until they are solid enough to stack. Then, place the falafels in an airtight container or bag between layers of greaseproof paper and freeze for up to 2 months. To cook from frozen, place on a lightly greased baking sheet, brush with oil and sprinkle the sesame seeds over the top. Bake as in the method for 25–30 minutes until cooked through and lightly golden.

Roasted celeriac laksa with lemongrass and lime

This is a gorgeous recipe that you will want to make again and again. It's not quite a traditional laksa, more an eminently slurpable soup full of warmth, fresh flavours and sunshine colours that are comforting and uplifting at the same time. Feel free to throw in some fresh noodles to warm through at the end if you are extra hungry. This recipe makes enough laksa paste for a second batch and is easy to freeze.

FEEDS 4

FOR THE LAKSA PASTE (MAKES DOUBLE)
60g coriander, roughly chopped
5 tbsp vegetable oil
6 garlic cloves, crushed
4 lemongrass stalks, trimmed, outer leaves
    removed, and very finely chopped
4 tbsp grated fresh ginger
3 red chillies, deseeded and roughly chopped
4 shallots, chopped
2 tsp turmeric
10 kaffir lime leaves, stems removed,
    very finely chopped (or crumbled if dried)
4 tbsp fish sauce

FOR THE CELERIAC
1 celeriac, peeled and halved
2 tbsp vegetable oil
2 garlic cloves
1 onion, finely sliced
2 leeks, sliced into thick discs
2 green peppers, deseeded and sliced
750ml vegetable stock
1 x 400ml tin of full- or reduced-fat
    coconut milk
finely grated zest and juice of 1 lime
light soy sauce, to taste
coriander leaves, to serve

1   First, make the paste. Add all the ingredients into a mini processor and blitz to a rough paste. Place half the laksa paste in a small airtight container and drizzle a thin layer of oil over the top. Seal and refrigerate for up to 3 days or freeze for up to 2 months. Set aside the remainder to use for the celeriac.

2   Preheat the oven to 220°C/200°C fan/ Gas mark 7 and grease 2 large baking trays.

3   Slice each celeriac half into 8 thick slices. Toss these with 1 tablespoon of the oil and 1 tablespoon of laksa paste and place on a baking tray. Roast for 20–25 minutes, turning halfway through, until tender throughout and browned around the edges. Remove from the oven and keep warm.

4   Heat the remaining oil in a large saucepan or wok over a medium–high heat and cook the garlic, onion and leeks quickly for 10–12 minutes until the vegetables are very soft, slightly golden but not burnt. Spoon in the remaining laksa paste and fry for 2 minutes. Toss in the peppers and cook for 1 minute, then pour in the vegetable stock and coconut milk.

5 Bring to a gentle simmer, without boiling, for 3 minutes, then add the roasted celeriac and warm through. Remove from the heat, stir in the lime zest and juice and season with soy sauce to taste. Serve sprinkled with the coriander leaves.

TO FREEZE
To freeze the finished celeriac laksa, allow it to cool completely, then transfer to an airtight container and freeze for up to 2 months. Defrost and reheat slowly, without boiling, until piping hot throughout.

Speedy spinach and feta triangles

These little pies are multi-taskers, equally at home in a lunchbox or served as pre-dinner munchies and light lunches. Unlike most spinach-pie recipes, here the raw spinach is 'cooked' by being gently crushed with a little salt, which helps to retain colour and texture. This recipe makes a large amount but the triangles will disappear fast, so make sure you stash away a few in the freezer before anyone else sees them! Here we are using tinned Eazy onions for speed, but the recipe works just as well with home-cooked.

MAKES 28–40 (DEPENDING ON PASTRY BRAND)

600g spinach, washed and roughly chopped
1 tsp salt
½ x 390g tin of Eazy onions, drained; or 1 onion, finely chopped and fried gently in 10g butter for 6–8 minutes until soft
200g feta cheese, crumbled
2 eggs, beaten
about 220g filo pastry sheets
50g butter, melted
2 tbsp olive oil
sesame seeds, for sprinkling
black pepper to season

1 If serving straight away, preheat the oven to 200°C/180°C fan/Gas mark 6, and place reusable liners or sheets of greaseproof paper on to 2 large baking sheets.

2 Place the spinach in a large colander and sprinkle it with the teaspoon of salt. Using your hands, massage the leaves and rip them into smaller pieces. The spinach will quickly start to break down and wilt. Carry on massaging until the volume of the spinach reduces by half. Squeeze out the liquid with your hands.

3 Tip the spinach, onions, crumbled feta and beaten eggs into a large mixing bowl. Season generously with black pepper and stir well.

4 Lay out the filo sheets and, using scissors, cut each sheet lengthways into 4 strips. Depending on the brand of filo, you will have between 20 and 36 strips.

5 Mix the butter with the olive oil. Brush a thin layer of the mixture over the first strip of filo.

6   Starting at the bottom of the first strip, place 2 tablespoons of spinach mixture in the centre. Fold the bottom-left hand corner of the filo strip over the filling to make a triangle. Continue folding the filled triangle up the strip until you reach the top and have a plump, filled triangle. Place on the greased baking sheet. Continue making triangles with the rest of the spinach mixture and filo strips until they are all used up. (See freezer notes now if you intend to freeze.)

7   To bake, paint the triangles with the last of the butter and oil mixture and sprinkle with sesame seeds. Bake for 20–25 minutes until crispy and golden.

TO FREEZE
Place the unbaked triangles between layers of cling film or reusable liners in an airtight bag or box and freeze for up to 1 month. Bake from frozen on a greased baking tray at 200°C/180°C fan/Gas mark 6 for 30–35 minutes until crisp and golden.

Chipotle, sun-dried tomato and sunshine pepper paella

This is a colourful, simple, happy and filling dish, packed with vegetables. It uses oil from a jar of sun-dried tomatoes, which is infused with warm, tomato-y flavours. Make the dish in advance and keep it in the fridge for 3 days, or freeze it and reheat it gently.

FEEDS 4

2 tbsp sun-dried tomato oil
1 small red onion, finely chopped
2 garlic cloves, crushed
1 large leek, sliced into thin discs
¼ tbsp chipotle paste
¼ tsp turmeric
¼ tsp smoked paprika
1 each of red, yellow and green peppers, deseeded and thinly sliced
200g paella rice
100ml sherry
500ml hot vegetable stock
8 sun-dried tomatoes in oil, drained and finely chopped
200g frozen peas
salt and black pepper to season
handful of flat-leaf parsley, leaves picked and chopped, to serve
1 lemon, quartered, to serve

1   Heat the oil in a lidded sauté pan or large, deep frying pan on a medium heat and cook the onion, garlic, leek, chipotle paste and spices gently for 8–10 minutes until the onion is soft and translucent. Add the peppers and fry for another 5 minutes.

2   Tip in the rice and stir thoroughly. Pour in the sherry and let it boil off before adding the hot stock. Stir well, then add the sun-dried tomatoes.

3   Bring to the boil, turn down to a gentle simmer and cover with a tight-fitting lid. Simmer for 25 minutes without peeking, then turn off the heat, stir in the frozen peas and put the lid back on for 4 minutes. Season to taste and serve scattered with chopped parsley, with lemon wedges on the side.

TO FREEZE
Allow the paella to cool completely before transferring to an airtight container and freezing for up to 2 months. Defrost and reheat slowly until piping hot throughout.

Squash, pine nut and harissa 'sausage' rolls

These are seriously feisty, vibrantly coloured and totally delicious little rolls that will put a rocket into your day. If you prefer things a little calmer, leave out the fresh chilli.

MAKES 16

750g butternut squash, peeled, deseeded
    and roughly chopped into 2cm chunks
2 red onions, halved
2 tbsp olive oil
1 red chilli, deseeded and finely chopped
4 tbsp pine nuts
1 tbsp harissa paste
1 ready-rolled sheet of puff pastry
1 egg, beaten
2 tsp sesame seeds
salt and black pepper to season

1 If serving straight away, preheat the oven to 200°C/180°C fan/Gas mark 6.

2 Combine the squash, onions, oil and chilli in a baking tray and season well. Roast for 40 minutes, stirring from time to time until the squash chunks are soft throughout and caramelised around the edges.

3 While the squash is roasting, toast the pine nuts in a dry frying pan on a medium–high heat until lightly golden (watch they don't burn!). Roughly chop and set aside.

4 Remove the baking tray from the oven, transfer the pieces of butternut squash to a mixing bowl and roughly mash.

5 Chop the roasted onion and tip it, along with any chilli bits and oil left in the baking tray, into the mixing bowl and mix well. Stir in the harissa and pine nuts and season to taste.

6 Unroll the puff pastry sheet on to a piece of greaseproof paper (or use the paper it comes wrapped in) and cut it in half down its length, into 2 strips. Halve the butternut mixture and use each half in turn to create a line of filling down the centre of each pastry strip.

7 One strip at a time, paint a line of beaten egg down one side, and bring the other side over to cover it. Press lightly to seal, then roll the 2 pastry tubes over so that the seams are underneath. Cut each length into 8 equal pieces, and place on a baking tray lined with greaseproof paper or a reusable liner. (See freezer notes now if you intend to freeze.)

8 When you are ready to cook, lightly brush the rolls with egg and scatter sesame seeds over the top. Bake for 25–30 minutes until the rolls are puffed up and gloriously golden. Eat warm for maximum tastiness.

TO FREEZE
Put the unbaked rolls between layers of greaseproof paper and place them in an airtight box or bag. Freeze for up to 2 months. To bake from frozen, lightly brush the rolls with egg and scatter sesame seeds over the top. Bake as in the method.

Parsnip and cumin rostis

These are big, chunky vegetable rostis that work equally well as an edible plate or as a simple side dish. If you have a burger press or crumpet ring you'll be able to create picture-perfect patties, but your hands will do the job just as well if you don't.

MAKES 8

500g parsnips, peeled
200g carrots, peeled
2 tbsp vegetable oil, for frying
1 tsp cumin seeds
1 tsp mustard seeds
1 large onion, finely chopped
1 tsp ground cumin
1 egg, beaten
3 tbsp gram or plain flour
2 tbsp chopped coriander, plus extra to serve
salt and black pepper to season

1 Bring a large saucepan of water to the boil. Add the whole parsnips and carrots and cook for 8 minutes. Drain and allow to cool.

2 While the vegetables are boiling, heat half the oil in a frying pan on a medium–high heat and add the cumin and mustard seeds. Fry until they start to pop, then turn the heat down, add the onion and cook gently for 8 minutes until translucent. Add the ground cumin, cook for another 2 minutes, and then tip into a large mixing bowl.

3 Add the egg, flour and coriander to the mixing bowl. Coarsely grate the parsnips and carrots on top, mix well and season generously with salt and pepper.

4 Using your hands or a burger press, form the mixture into 8 equal-sized patties. Place the patties between layers of greaseproof paper and chill for at least 1 hour, or overnight. (See freezer notes now if you intend to freeze.)

5 To cook, heat the remaining 1 tablespoon of oil in a non-stick frying pan over a medium heat. When the oil is hot, carefully place the rostis in the pan and cook for 5–6 minutes on each side until nicely golden and cooked through. Serve sprinkled with coriander and sea salt.

TO FREEZE
Place the uncooked rostis between layers of greaseproof paper in an airtight box or bag. Cook from frozen as in the recipe, but for 8 minutes on each side.

Stuffed gem squash with goat's cheese, walnuts and honey

What more perfect example of the ultimate zero-waste meal could you find than crockery you can eat? Gem squashes are nature's bowls, making them the ideal vessels for filling with your favourite flavours. Here, they are stuffed with a combination of crunchy nuts and pungent cheese and drizzled with honey. Prepare the squash halves up to 2 days in advance and store, covered, in the fridge before filling and baking.

FEEDS 8

8 young gem squashes
4 tbsp olive oil
8 thyme sprigs, leaves picked and chopped
100g walnuts, roughly chopped
300g soft, rindless goat's cheese or other soft cheese
1 tsp red pepper or chilli flakes
1–2 tbsp runny honey
salt and black pepper to season

1   Cut the squashes in half horizontally. Trim the stems slightly so the halves will sit flat. Remove the seeds and membrane from the centres and discard.

2   Bring a large pan of salted water to the boil and cook the squash halves for 8–10 minutes until tender. Drain and set aside. If you are making them in advance, allow the squash halves to cool completely before covering and refrigerating for up to 2 days.

3   To bake, preheat the oven to 200°C/180°C fan/ Gas mark 6 and grease a large baking tray.

4   Place the squash halves, cut sides upwards, on the baking tray. Brush the insides and tops of each half with olive oil and season generously with salt and pepper. Sprinkle over the chopped thyme leaves, then spoon half the walnuts and all the goat's cheese equally into the squashes. Scatter over the chilli flakes and remaining walnuts, season again and drizzle the honey evenly over the squashes.

5   Bake for 15–20 minutes until the squashes are tender and piping hot. Serve immediately.

Spiced red lentils with coconut and lime

Filling, tasty and comforting with an astonishing depth of flavour – this is vegan heaven in a bowl! It's more than enough for a good meal served up with grains or rice, or you can add a little water if you want to enjoy it as a soup.

FEEDS 6

2 tbsp coconut or vegetable oil
3 tsp cumin seeds
1 tsp fennel seeds
3 tsp mustard seeds
large bunch of coriander, leaves picked, stalks finely chopped
2 red onions, finely sliced
5 garlic cloves, crushed
¼ tsp chilli flakes
2 carrots, peeled and coarsely grated
2 tsp turmeric
400g red lentils
2 x 400g tins of chopped tomatoes
1 x 400ml tin of full- or reduced-fat coconut milk
2 tbsp finely grated fresh ginger
1 tsp salt, plus extra to season
generous grinding of black pepper, plus extra to season
finely grated zest and juice of 2 limes
1 red chilli, deseeded and thinly sliced (optional)

1 Heat the oil in a large sauté pan or heavy-bottomed saucepan on a medium–high heat and fry the cumin, fennel and mustard seeds until they start jumping.

2 Turn the heat down and add the chopped coriander stalks, along with the onions, garlic, chilli and carrots and cook for 10–12 minutes until they have softened. Stir in the turmeric and cook for another 2 minutes.

3 Pour in the lentils and add the tomatoes, 3 tins of water, the coconut milk and the grated fresh ginger. Stir in the teaspoon of salt and a generous grinding of pepper.

4 Bring to the boil and then reduce to a gentle simmer for 35–45 minutes until you have a thick, soupy consistency. Stir frequently, as lentils like to stick to the bottom of the pan.

5 Add the lime zest and juice and more salt and pepper if desired. Stir in half of the coriander leaves and sprinkle the rest over the top before serving.

TO FREEZE
Allow the stew to cool completely, then transfer to an airtight container (or containers if portioning). Freeze for up to 2 months. Defrost and reheat gently without boiling.

Herby butter bean and kale stew

Lots of fresh green herbs bring a clean and simple feel to this soothing vegan stew. Stir in a lively lemon and garlic flavourbomb before serving to give an extra blast of flavour. Great with a hunk of crusty bread.

FEEDS 4—6

FOR THE LEMON AND GARLIC FLAVOURBOMB

2 tbsp chopped flat-leaf parsley, plus extra
   to serve
finely grated zest of 1 lemon
1 garlic clove, crushed
1 tbsp olive oil
salt and black pepper to season

FOR THE STEW

2 tbsp olive oil
4 garlic cloves, crushed
3 celery sticks, finely chopped
1 large Spanish onion, quartered and
   finely sliced
50g kale, thinly sliced
1 tbsp finely chopped rosemary leaves
1 tsp dried oregano
3 sage leaves, finely chopped
big pinch of salt
3 tbsp wholegrain mustard
2 tsp runny honey
3 x 400g tins of butter beans
juice of 1 lemon

1   Combine all the flavourbomb ingredients and season with salt and pepper. Cover and set aside.

2   Heat the oil in a large sauté pan or deep frying pan on a medium heat. Tip in the garlic, celery, onion, kale and herbs. Add the big pinch of salt and cook gently for 10–12 minutes until the vegetables are soft.

3   Stir in the mustard, honey and butter beans, and add half a tin of water. Cook gently for 10 minutes until the beans are warmed through. Stir through the lemon juice and the flavourbomb, taste and add plenty of salt and pepper. Scatter with chopped parsley, if desired.

TO FREEZE

Allow to cool completely, then transfer to an airtight container and place in the freezer. Defrost completely before reheating slowly until piping hot throughout.

Sunny butternut and sweet potato gratin

This is a gorgeously uplifting bake, full of colourful vegetables and crunchy pine nuts in a sage-infused cheese sauce. It's a big, generous recipe that makes a luxurious vegetarian main course. You can prepare it up to 2 days in advance.

FEEDS 8

400ml double cream
300ml milk
4 garlic cloves, crushed
4 sage leaves, plus 2 tbsp chopped sage
6 black peppercorns
large pinch of paprika, plus extra for sprinkling
900g butternut squash, peeled, deseeded and
    very thinly sliced
600g sweet potato, peeled and thinly sliced
20g butter, plus extra for greasing
1 tbsp olive oil
1 large Spanish onion, finely chopped
30g pine nuts, toasted
120g Gruyère cheese, finely grated
salt and black pepper to season

1   Pour the cream and milk into a saucepan and add the garlic, 4 sage leaves, the peppercorns and paprika. Slowly bring to the boil, then remove from the heat and leave to infuse for 10 minutes.

2   Bring a large pan of salted water to the boil. Boil the butternut and sweet potato slices in batches for 5 minutes at a time, taking care not to overcrowd the pan. Drain and set aside.

3   Meanwhile, melt the butter in a frying pan over a medium heat with the olive oil, and fry the onion for 8–10 minutes until soft and translucent. Add 1 tablespoon of the chopped sage and fry for another 3 minutes.

4   Grease a large ovenproof dish and place alternating layers of butternut and sweet potato in the dish. Scatter over the onion and sprinkle over another pinch of paprika. Season very generously with salt and pepper.

5   Strain the infused cream mixture, and pour the strained liquid over the vegetables. Scatter over the pine nuts and grated Gruyère.

6   To cook, preheat the oven to 190°C/170°C fan/ Gas mark 5.

7   Bake for 50–60 minutes until bubbling and golden on top. Use a skewer to test whether the vegetables are cooked through, and cook for another 10–20 minutes if needed, covering loosely with foil if the top starts to burn. Remove from the oven, season again and allow to stand and 'set' for 10 minutes. Sprinkle with the remaining chopped sage and serve.

MAKE AHEAD
If you are making this dish in advance, cover it with foil and refrigerate for up to 2 days.

Fast and furious quinoa 'bolognese'

Traditional fillings for stuffed peppers and tomatoes tend to be rice- and meat-based, so this vegan version, created by my friend Polly, makes a welcome change. Thanks to the ready-cooked quinoa, it is quick to put together. Use it to stuff peppers, courgettes and tomatoes, or as a filling for lettuce and summer leaves.

FEEDS 4

2 tbsp olive oil
2 red onions, finely chopped
2 garlic cloves, crushed
small bunch of flat-leaf parsley, stalks and leaves finely chopped separately
2 courgettes, finely diced
3 tbsp chopped capers
2 tbsp tapenade or sun-dried tomato paste
1 x 400g tin of chopped tomatoes
generous pinch of sugar
250g sachet of ready-cooked quinoa
½ tsp salt, plus extra to season
4 tbsp pine nuts, toasted
4 large red peppers
black pepper to season

1   Heat the olive oil in a large, shallow pan over a medium heat and gently fry the onions, garlic and parsley stalks for 8–10 minutes until the onions are soft and translucent. Remove from the pan with a slotted spatula, increase the heat and fry the diced courgettes quickly until golden.

2   Return the onions to the pan and add the capers, paste, tomatoes, sugar and quinoa. Stir in the ½ teaspoon of salt and season with plenty of pepper. Cook for 10–12 minutes until the sauce thickens. Taste and add more seasoning if desired.

3   Remove from the heat and stir through the chopped parsley leaves and the pine nuts. (See freezer notes now if you intend to freeze.)

4   Preheat the oven to 180°C/160°C fan/ Gas mark 4.

5   Slice a 'lid' off the top of each of the peppers. Remove the seeds and white pith from the insides and rub the skins with olive oil. Stuff the peppers with the sauce and place in a greased baking tin. Cook for 30 minutes until piping hot, then serve.

TO FREEZE
To freeze the filling, allow to cool completely and freeze in airtight containers or bags for up to 2 months. Defrost completely before using as in the method.

The joy of batch baking sweets and treats is that they freeze remarkably well, so with a little preparation, you'll always have something naughty to hand when you need a sugar hit.

7 | Sweets and treats

There are a few useful guidelines to follow when you're aiming for sugary nirvana. First, go for bakes with staying power, such as traybakes, moist cakes, and tarts. These don't mind being frozen and hold their flavour and texture well (unlike Victoria sponges and fairy cakes, which are best eaten fresh). It's also a good idea to head for the garden as well as the store cupboard when you're choosing ingredients. Grated vegetables, such as carrot, beetroot and courgettes, make marvellously moist cakes, and even the most ardent vegetable hater won't notice you've included them! Making a big batch of loaf cakes is a great way to use up vegetable gluts, and they will happily freeze for a few months and yet still taste super-fresh.

The natural geometry of traybakes and bars lend themselves well to hassle-free batch baking. The square and rectangular baking tins create nice, even bakes that you can easily portion perfectly so that everyone gets an equal slice. Dense loaf cakes stack neatly in the freezer and are easy to cut into even slices. Make small cakes and cookies in muffin tins and freeze chocolate chip cookies uncooked in doughy dollops, ready to bake into warm, fresh, homemade cookies within 15 minutes of leaving the freezer. And some bakes, such as the Dark chocolate and fresh mint bars on page 190, are even better when eaten almost, but not quite, defrosted. The chill brings an exhilaratingly icy blast to the fresh mint icing and a satisfying chocolatey crunch.

Dive into this chapter and treat yourself to a sugar-dusted baking session, creating tantalising make-ahead bakes. From the dark and serious treasure-filled Date and stem ginger loaf (see p.201) to a heavenly batch of Ridiculously good Toblerone brownies (p.202), fill your house with divine wafts of cinnamon, vanilla and chocolate and make everyone smile with these utterly irresistible sweet treats.

The best batch sweets and treats

One-bowl spiced apple and almond cake

Blueberry and lemon crumble bars

Passion fruit and ginger mini-cheesecakes

Citrusy apricot and carrot traybake

Pear and pistachio frangipane tart

Beetroot, cranberry and walnut loaves

Dark chocolate and fresh mint bars

White chocolate and sour cherry cookies

Courgette, lime and pistachio loaves

Monster autumn fruit crumble

Sorbet-stuffed frozen oranges

Date and stem ginger loaf

Ridiculously good Toblerone brownies

One-bowl spiced apple and almond cake

This is the easiest cake in the world. It's prepared in one bowl and works every time so it's easy on the washing-up too. It bakes long and slow, and must be left alone to cool completely in the tin, but I promise it's worth the wait.

FEEDS 8

4 eating apples, peeled, cored and finely diced
¼ tsp mixed spice
½ tsp ground cinnamon, plus extra for decorating
175g butter
175g self-raising flour
175g caster sugar, plus extra for decorating
3 eggs, beaten
1 tsp almond essence
20g flaked almonds

1   Preheat the oven to 170°C/150°C fan/ Gas mark 3.

2   Grease a 24cm round cake tin (or similar) and line it with greaseproof paper or a reusable liner.

3   Place all the ingredients except the flaked almonds into a large bowl and mix well. Pour the cake mixture into the prepared tin and sprinkle the almonds evenly over the top.

4   Mix a pinch of cinnamon with a tablespoon of caster sugar and sprinkle the mixture over the top of the cake.

5   Bake for 50–60 minutes until lightly golden and a skewer inserted into the centre comes out clean. Remove from the oven and cool in the tin for at least 30 minutes before serving.

TO FREEZE
Cool completely, wrap in greaseproof paper and place in an airtight box or bag in the freezer. Defrost before serving.

Blueberry and lemon crumble bars

With a lemon shortbread base, deep purple, jammy blueberry centre and a crunchy crumble topping, this is a more-ish traybake that keeps and freezes well.

MAKES 16 CROWD-PLEASING PIECES

FOR THE SHORTBREAD BASE
120g butter
60g caster sugar
finely grated zest of 1 lemon
175g plain flour

FOR THE FILLING
200g blueberries
3 tbsp lemon juice
1½ tbsp cornflour
50g caster sugar

FOR THE CRUMBLE TOPPING
50g butter
80g plain flour
50g caster sugar

1   Preheat the oven to 180°C/160°C fan/ Gas mark 4 and grease and line a 20cm x 20cm baking tin.

2   First, make the shortbread. Beat the butter, sugar and lemon zest together until light and fluffy. Add the flour and knead gently until you have a crumbly dough. Tip the dough into the lined tin and flatten so that the top is smooth and even. Prick the dough all over with a fork. Bake for 20 minutes until slightly golden, then leave to cool in the tin.

3   While the shortbread is baking, make the filling. Place the blueberries in a small saucepan with the 3 tablespoons of lemon juice. Bring to the boil then reduce the heat and simmer for 4–5 minutes so that the berries begin to break down.

4   Mix the cornflour and sugar together and stir the mixture into the blueberries until everything thickens and stiffens. Set aside to cool while you make the crumble topping.

5   Rub the butter into the flour until it has the texture of fine breadcrumbs. Stir in the sugar.

6   Pour the cooled blueberry mixture over the shortbread base and scatter the crumble evenly over the top. Bake for 40–45 minutes until golden-brown. Cool for 10 minutes in the tin, then score into 16 pieces. Remove from the tin and cool on a wire rack. Delicious warm or cold.

TO FREEZE
Cool completely and wrap in foil before freezing for up to 2 months.

Passion fruit and ginger mini-cheesecakes

Mini-cheesecakes are great for batch baking as you can make and freeze them in advance and defrost an hour before serving. Here, passion fruit brings vibrant colours and summery flavours to a lively gingernut base. Using a muffin tin ensures you'll have perfect-sized portions.

MAKES 12

250g gingernut biscuits
120g butter, softened
400g full-fat cream cheese
150g caster sugar
1 tsp vanilla essence
3 eggs, beaten
juice of 4 passion fruits

1   Preheat the oven to 160°C/140°C fan/Gas mark 2–3 and place 12 paper cake cases into a 12-hole muffin tin.

2   Whizz the gingernuts into small crumbs in a food processor. Add the softened butter and process for a little longer until combined.

3   Divide the crumb mixture equally between the cases and, using the bottom of a bottle, press down gently into each case so the crumbs are completely flat.

4   In a large mixing bowl, beat the cream cheese, caster sugar and vanilla essence together. Gradually add the eggs, one at a time, and then pour over the passion-fruit juice, stirring it through just once, so that the juice swirls are visible.

5   Divide the cheesecake mixture equally between the biscuit cases, and use a cocktail stick or skewer to swirl through the bright orange juice a little more.

6   Bake for 35 minutes until just firm. Allow to cool completely before refrigerating for at least 4 hours.

TO FREEZE
Allow to cool completely, then transfer to an airtight container and freeze for up to 2 months.

Citrusy apricot and carrot traybake

This is a really useful recipe for a deep, moist carrot traybake that you can make in advance and freeze until needed. It's packed with traditional spices and citrus-soaked fruit. Most carrot cakes are topped with a cream-cheese icing, but this recipe uses a tart lemon icing, which contrasts nicely with the dense cake.

FEEDS 16

finely grated zest and juice of 1 orange
100g apricots, chopped
220g self-raising flour
1 tsp baking powder
½ tsp bicarbonate of soda
2 tsp ground cinnamon
1½ tsp mixed spice
180g carrots, peeled and finely grated
50g walnuts, chopped
finely grated zest of 1 lemon
4 eggs
160ml sunflower oil
180g light brown soft sugar

FOR THE ICING
250g icing sugar
juice of 1 lemon

1 Preheat the oven to 180°C/160°C fan/Gas mark 4 and grease and line a 20cm x 20cm baking tin with greaseproof paper or a reusable liner.

2 Place the orange zest into a large mixing bowl and pour the juice into a small saucepan. Add the chopped apricots to the saucepan and bring to the boil. Turn off the heat, stir and leave to cool.

3 Add the flour, baking powder, bicarbonate of soda, cinnamon, mixed spice, carrots, walnuts and lemon zest to the mixing bowl and mix well. Stir in the cooled apricots and any liquid from the saucepan.

4 In a separate bowl, whisk the eggs, oil and sugar together until completely combined. Tip into the dry ingredients and mix well.

5 Pour the cake mixture into the lined baking tin and bake for 40–45 minutes until a skewer inserted into the centre comes out clean and the top bounces back when lightly pressed. Leave to cool in the tin for 5 minutes, then take the paper off and leave to cool completely on a wire rack. (See freezer notes now if you intend to freeze the traybake.)

6 When the cake is cold, whisk the icing sugar and lemon juice together until you have a soft dropping consistency. Pour on to the cake and smooth with a knife. For extra impact, sprinkle some extra walnuts and apricots on the icing before it sets.

TO FREEZE
Cool the cake completely. Do not ice. Wrap tightly in cling film and then a layer of foil and freeze for up to 2 months.

Pear and pistachio frangipane tart

I developed this tart to use up a few slightly bruised windfalls, but it exceeded all expectations. Now it's a perfect, posh pudding or afternoon treat, and I've even taken little slices on a long winter's walk to keep any flaggers motivated. It freezes well, so make it when you too have fruit hanging around, and bank it for a day when your table is full of hungry people. It will keep for 2–3 days in the fridge.

FEEDS 6–8

FOR THE PASTRY
220g plain flour, plus extra for rolling
50g caster sugar
110g butter

FOR THE FILLING
120g pistachios, chopped
140g butter
140g caster sugar
2 eggs, beaten
½ tsp almond extract
2 tbsp plain flour
350g pears, peeled, cored and cut into slices
icing sugar, for dusting

1 To make the pastry, place the flour, sugar and butter in a food processor and pulse until it resembles fine breadcrumbs. Gradually add 3–4 tablespoons of cold water until the mixture forms a large ball.

2 Grease a 22cm loose-bottomed tart tin.

3 Knead the dough lightly on a floured surface, and roll into a circle slightly larger than the tart tin. Lay the dough over the tin and press to fit. Roughly trim the top, leaving a slight overlap (it will shrink as it bakes). Prick the base with a fork and chill for 30 minutes.

4 Preheat the oven to 180°C/160°C fan/ Gas mark 4 and place a large baking tray inside.

5 Line the chilled tart case with baking paper and fill with baking beans. Blind bake for 15 minutes, then remove the paper and beans and bake for another 15 minutes until lightly golden.

6 Remove the tart case from the oven and make the filling while it cools.

7 Set aside a tablespoon of pistachios for decorating the tart. Place the rest in a food processor and blitz until ground. Set aside.

8 Cream the butter and sugar together until fluffy, and gradually add the eggs and then add the almond extract. Fold in the flour and ground pistachios with a spoon.

9 Spoon into the cooled tart case and smooth the top. Place the pear slices in an overlapping circle evenly across the frangipane, and press them slightly into the filling. Bake for 40–50 minutes until beautifully golden, covering loosely with foil after 30 minutes if it looks as if the top is browning too fast.

10 Remove from the oven, scatter with the remaining chopped pistachios and leave to cool on a wire rack for 15 minutes. When it is cool enough, dust with icing sugar and serve.

TO FREEZE AFTER BAKING
Cool the tart completely and wrap in cling film or foil. To serve warm, defrost and heat in a preheated oven at 180°C/160°C fan/Gas mark 4 for 35–45 minutes until piping hot, covering with foil after 20 minutes if the top looks as if it is starting to burn.

Beetroot, cranberry and walnut loaves

This is a surprising cake that doesn't taste of beetroot at all. It's just a very rich and chocolatey, moist cake that happens to include a few vegetables. It's good at any time of year, but particularly nice in winter, when it makes a great alternative to heavy fruit cakes. Because it's so moist, it also freezes very well, so this recipe handily makes 2 hearty loaves.

250g beetroot
3 eggs
220ml sunflower oil
400g caster sugar
1 tsp vanilla essence
250g courgette, coarsely grated
60g cocoa powder
300g plain flour
3 tsp baking powder
2 tsp bicarbonate of soda
½ tsp salt
100g dried cranberries
100g walnuts, chopped, plus extra
    for decorating

OPTIONAL CREAM-CHEESE ICING (PER CAKE)
80g full-fat cream cheese
200g icing sugar, sifted
finely grated zest and juice of 1 orange

1   Preheat the oven to 170°C/150°C fan/Gas mark 3 and line 2 large (900g) loaf tins with greaseproof paper or reusable liners.

2   Place the unpeeled beetroot in the microwave and cook until soft (6–9 minutes depending on size). (Alternatively, bake in the oven at 180°C/160°F fan/Gas mark 4 for 60–70 minutes until the beetroot is tender.) Peel, then coarsely grate into a large bowl.

3   Tip the eggs, oil, sugar, vanilla and grated courgettes into the bowl with the beeroot and mix well.

4   In another bowl, combine the cocoa powder, flour, baking powder, bicarbonate of soda and salt. Tip the mixture into the cake batter and combine.

5   Mix in the cranberries and walnuts, and then pour the mixture equally into the lined loaf tins.

6   Cook for 50–55 minutes until nicely risen and a skewer inserted into the centre comes out clean.

7 Remove the cakes from the oven and place them in their tins on a cooling rack for 10 minutes. Remove from the tins and allow to cool completely in their greaseproof wraps. (See freezer notes now if you intend to freeze the cake.)

8 To ice, mix the cream cheese, icing sugar, orange zest and a tablespoon of orange juice together, adding more icing sugar if the mixture is too wet. Do not overbeat. Spread over the cake and allow to set. Decorate with walnuts before serving.

TO FREEZE

Cool the cake completely. Do not ice. Wrap tightly in cling film and then in a layer of foil and freeze for up to 2 months.

Dark chocolate and fresh mint bars

These taste like a shortbread version of After Eights! If you can find fresh peppermint leaves, use them, if not, bolster the minty-ness with a little peppermint essence.

MAKES 20–25

120g butter
60g caster sugar
175g plain flour
160g icing sugar
2 tbsp finely chopped peppermint leaves;
    or 1 tbsp fresh mint leaves, finely chopped,
    plus 1 tsp peppermint essence
200g dark cooking chocolate (at least
    36% cocoa solids)
extra mint leaves, to decorate

1   Preheat the oven to 180°C/160°C fan/Gas mark 4. Line a 20cm x 20cm baking tin with a large sheet of greaseproof paper or a reusable liner that overlaps the sides. This will help to remove the bars when set.

2   Beat the butter and sugar together until light and fluffy. Gradually mix in the flour to form a crumbly dough. Press all the crumbs together into a ball and press it into the baking tin. Smooth the dough so it is completely even. Prick it gently all over with a fork and bake for 20–25 minutes until golden. Leave to cool in the tin.

3   Make the peppermint filling by mixing the icing sugar with a little water until you have a stiff paste with no lumps. Add the fresh mint leaves and either the peppermint essence (if you are using it) or a little more water until you have a stiff icing that only just drops off a spoon.

4   Smooth over the top of the cooled shortbread and allow to set.

5   Break the chocolate into squares and place in a heatproof bowl over a pan of simmering water. Do not allow the bottom of the bowl to touch the water. Leave to melt, stirring as little as possible. When the chocolate has melted, pour it over the iced shortbread and tilt the tin from side to side so that it covers the top of the filling (you can use a palette knife here, but if you can do without, you will have a smoother top).

6   Allow to cool and then refrigerate until the chocolate has set. Remove from the tin and cut into 20–25 squares.

TO FREEZE

Wrap in in a layer of cling film followed by a layer of foil. Freeze for up to 2 months.

White chocolate and sour cherry cookies

If you're bored with traditional chocolate chip cookies, try these and you'll be well rewarded for your adventurous nature. White chocolate can be very sweet, but here it's used sparingly and matched with sour cherries, creating a perfectly balanced and satisfyingly chewy cookie. Cookie dough conveniently freezes, so you can save half of it for those days when you need something indulgent and you need it now!

MAKES 16

175g butter
120g caster sugar
80g light brown soft sugar
1 tsp vanilla essence
1 tbsp milk
1 egg, plus 1 egg yolk
225g plain flour
1 tsp bicarbonate of soda
50g sour cherries, snipped into small pieces
   with scissors
50g white chocolate, finely chopped

1 Preheat the oven to 180°C/160°C fan/Gas mark 4 and grease and line 2 baking trays with greaseproof paper or reusable liners.

2 Beat the butter with a hand or stand mixer until pale and creamy. Add the sugars, vanilla and milk and beat until fluffy, then gradually add the egg and egg yolk, beating until completely combined.

3 Mix the flour and bicarbonate of soda together and beat in a little at a time, until you have a stiff dough.

4 Tip in the cherries and white chocolate and mix gently through the dough.

5 If you are baking all the cookies immediately, dollop 16 equal-sized mounds of cookie dough on to the trays, making sure to leave as much space as possible between the mounds. Press the tops down to flatten slightly. (See freezer notes now if you intend to freeze the dough.)

6 Bake for 15–18 minutes until just turning golden around the edges if you like your cookies quite chewy. If you prefer them a little firmer, give them another 2 minutes. Remove from the oven and leave to cool for a few minutes before easing them on to a cooling rack.

TO FREEZE
Place the baking tray with the uncooked cookie mounds in the freezer for 40–50 minutes until solid. Remove from the freezer and slide the mounds into a freezer bag or box. To cook, simply place the frozen cookie mounds on a baking tray lined with greaseproof paper or a reusable liner and bake at 180°C/160°C fan/ Gas mark 4 for 18–20 minutes until crispy and brown around the edges. Remove from the oven and leave to cool for a few minutes before easing on to a cooling rack.

Courgette, lime and pistachio loaves

This is a fast and delicious, almost one-bowl recipe that is especially good in the summer, when courgettes are cheap and plentiful. Courgettes bring moistness but not flavour to a bake, so if you're feeding those who aren't usually fans, don't tell them! This freezable recipe makes 2 large loaf cakes.

4 eggs
220ml vegetable oil
350g caster sugar
finely grated zest of 2 limes
400g small courgettes, coarsely grated
440g self-raising flour
2 tsp baking powder
½ tsp salt

FOR THE ICING (PER CAKE)
200–250g icing sugar, sifted
1–2 tbsp lime juice
20g chopped or slivered pistachio nuts

1   Preheat the oven to 170°C/150°C fan/ Gas mark 3, and line 2 large (900g) loaf tins with greaseproof paper or reusable liners.

2   Mix the eggs, oil, sugar, zest and grated courgettes in a large mixing bowl.

3   Combine the flour, baking powder and salt together in a separate bowl, and then stir this into the courgette mixture. Divide the mixture equally between the loaf tins.

4   Bake for 45–50 minutes, until the tops are golden and springy, and a skewer inserted into the centres comes out clean.

5   Remove the cakes from the oven and leave in the tins for 10 minutes, then remove from the tins, peel away the paper and transfer to a wire rack to cool completely. (See freezer notes now if you intend to freeze.)

6   To ice, mix the icing sugar and lime juice together until you have a soft, dropping consistency and smooth this evenly over the cake. While the icing is still wet, sprinkle over the pistachio slivers. Allow to set before serving.

TO FREEZE
Cool the cakes completely. Don't ice. Wrap tightly in cling film and then in a layer of foil and freeze for up to 2 months.

Monster autumn fruit crumble

This is a mega-crumble, which makes an ideal pudding for a big gathering, or for siphoning into a mountain of yummy batches to enjoy all by your sneaky little self. It's not fussy, so if you're lucky enough to have some windfall apples and pears or some that aren't quite sparkly enough for eating, this is the recipe to turn to. The rich and crunchy crumble topping is made with roasted hazelnuts. Make the dish up to 2 days in advance, or freeze it unbaked ready to pull out and bake on cue.

FEEDS A WHOPPING 10–12

FOR THE FILLING
butter, for greasing
2.5kg mixed apples and pears, peeled,
    cored and cut into big chunks
130g light brown soft sugar
finely grated zest and juice of 2 lemons
1 tsp ground cinnamon
1 tsp vanilla essence

FOR THE TOPPING
160g diced butter
320g plain flour
100g white sugar
60g light brown soft sugar
60g roasted hazelnuts, chopped

1   Preheat the oven to 180°C/160°C fan/Gas mark 4 and grease a large ovenproof baking dish.

2   Make the filling. Place the fruit in the baking dish and add the sugar, lemon zest and juice, cinnamon and vanilla. Mix well, cover with foil and bake for 30 minutes. Allow to cool.

3   To make the topping, place the butter and flour in a mixing bowl and rub together with your fingertips to the texture of fine bread-crumbs. Stir in the sugars and hazelnuts. Scatter the topping evenly over the fruit. (You can keep the crumble, covered, like this for up to 2 days in the fridge, or see freezer notes now if you intend to freeze.)

4   If cooking straight away, bake for 60–70 minutes for the large crumble until the top is lightly golden and the fruit filling is starting to bubble around the edges. (Alternatively, make the crumble in individual portions, spooning the baked fruit into smaller dishes, scattering with crumble and baking for 25–30 minutes until golden.)

TO FREEZE
Wrap the assembled (but unbaked) crumble dish in foil and freeze for up to 2 months. Defrost and bake as in the method.

Sorbet-stuffed frozen oranges

Sorbet-stuffed fruits taste just like a summer holiday, so this recipe ensures you can have those sunshine flavours all year round. It's very easy, but does require regular stirring during the freezing process, so it's a good one to make when you know you will be home for a while.

MAKES 8 ORANGE SORBETS

10 large oranges
100–200ml shop-bought orange juice, if needed
100g caster sugar

1   Slice a large 'lid' from the top quarter of 8 oranges. Using your hands and a small, sharp knife, remove the flesh from the lids and bases of the oranges without damaging the shape of the shells.

2   Squeeze the juice out of the orange centres into a measuring jug, using your hands or a juicer. Cut the remaining oranges in half and squeeze their juice into the jug. You will need about 800ml of orange juice to fill the oranges, so top the jug up with shop-bought orange juice if you don't have enough from the oranges.

3   Place the sugar and 100ml of orange juice from the jug into a small saucepan and heat gently, stirring continuously until the sugar has completely dissolved. Cool for 10 minutes, then add the remaining juice from the jug.

4   Place the orange mixture into a freezer-friendly container (with a lid) and freeze for 1 hour. Remove from the freezer and whisk lightly with a fork to break up any ice crystals. Freeze for another 1 hour, then whisk again. Repeat the process twice more (another 2 hours), then spoon the sorbet into the orange skins and top with an orange lid. Place in an airtight container or freezer bag and freeze for another 1–2 hours until set. Remove from the freezer 15 minutes before you want to eat the sorbets.

Date and stem ginger loaf

Don't be fooled by the unassuming appearance of this stealth cake. This is a dark and grown-up loaf with a toffee-like sweetness and buried treasure in the form of little pockets of golden ginger hiding in its depths.

MAKES 1 LARGE LOAF

250g chopped dates
50g butter
½ tsp bicarbonate of soda
130g caster sugar
2 eggs, beaten
40g stem ginger, finely chopped, plus
   1 tablespoon of syrup from the jar
150g self-raising flour

1   Preheat the oven to 170°C/150°C fan/Gas mark 3 and line a large loaf tin with greaseproof paper or a reusable liner.

2   Put the dates into a saucepan with 250ml of water over a medium heat. Cook for 5 minutes, stirring continuously, until the water has been absorbed and you have a loose purée. Take the pan off the heat, stir in the butter and bicarbonate of soda and leave to cool.

3   In a large bowl, mix together the sugar, eggs, ginger and syrup. Pour in the date mixture, then the flour, and stir to combine. Pour into the lined tin.

4   Bake for 40 minutes, then cover the top loosely with foil and bake for another 25–30 minutes, until a skewer inserted into the centre comes out clean.

5   Leave to cool in the tin for 15 minutes, then transfer to a cooling rack to cool completely.

TO FREEZE

Wrap the loaf tightly in cling film and then a layer of foil and freeze for up to 2 months.

Ridiculously good Toblerone brownies

It's hard to improve on a brownie, but Toblerone brings extra crunch and chewiness to what is already close to perfection. Just one tip: when the cooking time is up, try to resist the temptation to eat the brownies while they are hot, because, amazingly, they get even better as they cool.

MAKES 25

175g butter
80g dark cooking chocolate (at least
    36% cocoa solids), broken into squares
100g milk chocolate, broken into squares
320g caster sugar
3 eggs, beaten
150g plain flour
4 chunks of Toblerone from a 150g bar,
    chopped into small chips

1   Preheat the oven to 170°C/150°C fan/Gas mark 3 and line a 20cm x 20cm square baking tin with greaseproof paper or a reusable liner.

2   Bring a saucepan half-filled with water to the boil, then turn down to a simmer. Place the butter and both chocolates in a heatproof bowl on top of the pan, making sure the bottom of the bowl doesn't touch the water. Stir the chocolate and butter together as they melt.

3   Remove the bowl from the heat and stir in the sugar, then the beaten eggs, followed by the flour. Add half the chopped Toblerone and stir once.

4   Tip the brownie mixture into the lined tin and scatter the remaining Toblerone over the top. Bake for 55 minutes until the top is firm, but the brownies still have a slight wobble in the middle, then remove from the oven and place the tin on a wire cooling rack. Allow to cool before cutting into squares.

TO FREEZE
Wrap the squares in foil and freeze for up to 2 months.

Index

C

Notes